Flankers
The New Generation

Yefim Gordon

Original translation by Dmitriy Komissarov

Midland Publishing

Flankers
The New Generation
© 2001 Yefim Gordon
ISBN 1 85780 121 0

Published by Midland Publishing
4 Watling Drive, Hinckley
LE10 3EY, England
Tel: 01455 254 490 Fax: 01455 254 495
E-mail: midlandbooks@compuserve.com

Midland Publishing is an imprint of
Ian Allan Publishing Ltd

Worldwide distribution (except North America):
Midland Counties Publications
4 Watling Drive, Hinckley
LE10 3EY, England
Telephone: 01455 233 747 Fax: 01455 233 737
E-mail: midlandbooks@compuserve.com

North American trade distribution:
Specialty Press Publishers & Wholesalers Inc.
11605 Kost Dam Road, North Branch, MN 55056
Tel: 651 583 3239 Fax: 651 583 2023
Toll free telephone: 800 895 4585

Design concept and layout by
Polygon Press Ltd
Colour artwork by Valentin Vetlitskiy

Printed in England by
Ian Allan Printing Ltd
Riverdene Business Park, Molesey Road,
Hersham, Surrey, KT12 4RG

This book has been jointly prepared
with Polygon Press Ltd, Moscow

The Su-30KI makes a spectacular landing after a demonstration flight.

Contents

In writing this book the author made use of unclassified information published in various sources, as well as press releases of Russian aerospace companies and recordings of press conferences held at various international airshows.

This book is illustrated with photographs by Yefim Gordon, Viktor Drooshlyakov, Pavel Maslov, Sergey Skrynnikov, Sergey Pashkovskiy, Aleksandr Barykin, Sergey Balakleyev, Katsuhiko Tokunaga, Helmut Walther, the Sukhoi OKB, KnAAPO, IAPO and the ITAR-TASS news agency.

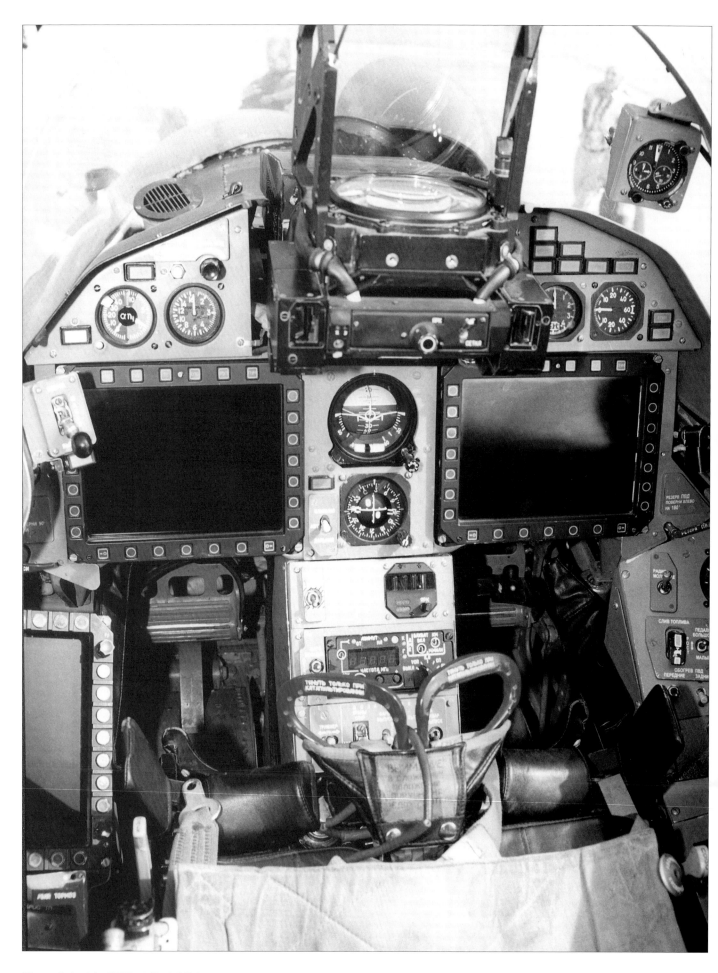

The cockpit of the T10M-11 (Su-37) fighter prototype. This is s typical example of how the cockpit of a Sukhoi 'Generation 4+' fighter's cockpit looks.

A New Generation of Flankers

Advanced Versions of the Sukhoi Su-27 Fighter

There is hardly another modern combat aircraft which is as popular with the press as the Flanker. Since the early 1980s when its existence came to light, the Sukhoi Su-27, one of the best fourth-generation fighters, has been the subject of dozens of books and hundreds of newspaper and magazine features. In case the reader does not know, the first prototype of Sukhoi's fourth-generation fighter designated T10-1 (called Flanker-A in the West) entered flight test on 20th May 1977. Sukhoi engineers, however, were not satisfied with the test results and a massive redesign ensued. Bearing the manufacturer's designation T10-S (*sereeynyy* – production, used attributively), the definitive design which gained worldwide fame as the Su-27 Flanker-B took to the air on 20th April 1981, exactly three years and eleven months after the original T-10; this was the seventh prototype (T10-7). Production aircraft started rolling off the assembly line in 1982.

Nearly twenty years have elapsed since then. Within this time span the design bureau named after Pavel Osipovich Sukhoi (OKB-51) has developed the Su-27 into a range of advanced and specialised single- and two-seat versions, many of which belong to the so-called Generation 4+. This was a joint effort with the engine design bureau named after Arkhip Mikhailovich Lyul'ka (now NPO Lyul'ka-Saturn). A major contribution was also made by the factories building the Flanker family – No. 126 in Komsomol'sk-on-Amur (KnAAPO), No. 39 in Irkutsk (IAPO) and No. 153 in Novosibirsk (NAPO).

(OKB = *opytno-konstrooktorskoye byuro* – experimental design bureau; the number is a code allocated for security reasons. NPO = *naoochno-proizvodstvennoye obyedineniye* – scientific & production association. KnAAPO = *Komsomol'skoye-na-Amoore aviatseeonnoye proizvodstvennoye obyedineniye* – Komsomol'sk-on-Amur Aircraft Production Association named after Yuriy A. Gagarin. IAPO = *Irkootskoye APO* – Irkutsk Aircraft Production. NAPO = *Novoseebeerskoye APO* – Novosibirsk Aircraft Production Association named after Valeriy P. Chkalov.)

The T10-24 control configured vehicle (CCV) undergoing conversion at Sukhoi's experimental plant.

Much has been written about the advanced versions of the Su-27. This book is an attempt to give an overview of the Generation 4+. Since the aircraft in question had separate designations commencing with a 3 (Su-30, Su-33 and so on), they may justifiably be called the 'Su-30 series'.

Once the general operational requirement (GOR) and specific operational requirement (SOR) for a new aircraft have been formulated and the development process begins, the aerodynamicists lead the way. The Su-27 was no exception: early attempts to enhance the fighter's capabilities centred on aerodynamics. Various versions, including those with aerodynamic improvements, were developed at a very early design stage. For instance, in 1977, when the basic T10-S was still unflown, Sukhoi engineers considered fitting all-movable canard foreplanes to the Su-27; however, wind tunnel tests showed the canards would cause pitch control problems at certain AoAs.

A wind tunnel model of the T10-M at TsAGI.

Above and below: The port engine of the LL-UV (PS) CCV featured a two-dimensional vectoring nozzle in a large boxy extension.

It took five years to cure the problem and a satisfactory canard design was brought out in 1982. The canards were positioned just aft of the cockpit on the wing leading-edge root extensions (LERXes); they had a 6.4-m (21 ft) span, an area of some 3 m² (32.25 sq. ft) and a leading-edge sweep of 53°30'.

The first Flanker to feature canards was the 24th development aircraft which bore the in-house designation T10-24. Aptly coded 24 Blue, the aircraft was completed in early 1985 by converting an early-production Su-27 (construction number unknown, fuselage number 07-01 – ie, Batch 7, first aircraft in the batch) and made its first flight in May. (**Note:** Unlike Western military aircraft (which have serials allowing positive identification), Soviet/CIS military aircraft usually have two-digit tactical codes which are simply the aircraft's number in the unit operating it.)

Tests showed that generally the canards worked as they should, improving field per-

formance and giving better handling at high angles of attack (AoAs, or alpha). They turned out to be a valuable asset at certain AoAs when the all-movable stabilizers (stabilators) found themselves in the wake of the wings and became inefficient. The canards were integrated into the fighter's digital fly-by-wire (FBW) control system and programmed to deflect automatically as alpha increased. They increased the aircraft's static instability, reducing trim drag and allowing the T10-24 to pull higher Gs without requiring the wing and horizontal tail structure to be reinforced.

The canards enhanced the T10-24's pitch and roll stability and control at high alpha. Moreover, by carefully choosing their position relative to the wings to create favourable airflow interference, Sukhoi engineers obtained a much bigger increase in lift than would have been provided by the canards alone. In a nutshell, the canards improved the Su-27's aerodynamics in many ways. The results were so

impressive that the new feature was incorporated into several new versions of the Flanker then under development (described later).

Meanwhile, the Sukhoi OKB was working on an even more agile fighter – the company's vision of the Soviet Union's fifth-generation fighter. This was a joint effort with several research establishments; eg, the Siberian Aviation Research Institute named after S. A. Chaplygin (SibNIA – *See**beer**skiy na**ooch**no-is**sled**ovatel'skiy insti**toot** avi**ah**tsii*) in Novosibirsk considered mating forward-swept wings to the Su-27. The know-how gained in the course of these programmes enabled Sukhoi to designing the world's first FSW supersonic fighter.

Several testbeds were used to verify the new aerodynamic features, avionics and systems which later found use on advanced versions of the Flanker. In 1985 the Sukhoi OKB started modification work on the second prototype Su-27UB Flanker-C combat trainer, the T10U-2 (02 Blue, c/n unknown, f/n 02-01). (UB = *oo**cheb**no-boye**voy** [samo**lyot**] – combat trainer.) The aircraft was fitted with a fully retractable L-shaped refuelling probe in order to test the Su-27's suitability for in-flight refuelling (IFR) and investigate crew workloads and physical condition on long-range missions. The probe was installed ahead of the windscreen, offset to port, with appropriate changes to the fuel system. Huge black and white phototheodolite calibration markings were added to the fins and nose.

The cockpits of the Su-27UB were carefully designed, with conveniently located controls; thus, with IFR capability, long missions would not be a problem. This was demonstrated in June 1987 when the aircraft made an unprecedented non-stop cross-country flight from Moscow to Komsomol'sk-on-Amur with Sukhoi OKB test pilots Nikolay F. Sadovnikov and Igor' Votintsev at the controls. Piloted by the same crew, the aircraft flew from Moscow to Komso-mol'sk-on-Amur and back in March 1988, covering 13,440 km (7,466 nm) in 15 hours 42 minutes. This flight included four top-ups from an Il'yushin Il-78 *Midas* tanker near Novosibirsk and Chita; the fairly frequent contacts with the tanker were caused by the need to drill refuelling techniques, not by the fighter running low on fuel.

Shortly afterwards, escorted by IA PVO (*Istrebitel'naya aviahtsiya **protivovozdoosh**noy oboro**ny*** – Air Defence Force fighter component) Su-27P interceptors, the aircraft paid a visit to the world's northernmost airfield, Graham-Bell airbase on the Zemlya Frantsa-Iosifa (Franz Josef Land) archipelago in the Barents Sea near the North Pole. This showed that the Flanker was well suited to the harsh climate of the Far North.

When the IFR system tests had been successfully completed, the T10U-2 was modified again under the Su-27K shipboard fighter programme by installing an arrestor

Above and below: The port engine of the LL-UV (PS) CCV featured a two-dimensional vectoring nozzle in a large boxy extension.

The T10U-2, suitably modified with an arrestor hook, catches the arrestor wire at Novofyodorovka.

The LMK-2405 CCV was used to verify a fly-by-wire control system featuring a side-stick.

hook under the tail 'stinger'. It underwent carrier suitability trials on a special test installation at the Soviet Navy's Flight Test Centre at Novofyodorovka AB, Saki (see Su-27K entry). The trials involved ski-jump take-offs and deck landings with an arrestor system. Besides, the two-seater served as an avionics testbed for the on-board components of the Resistor automatic carrier approach system. Later, when the first prototype Su-27K (T10K-1) commenced flight tests, the T10U-2 was equipped with an UPAZ-1A 'buddy' refuelling pod to act as a tanker for the naval fighter. (UPAZ = *oonifitseerovannyy podvesnoy agregaht zaprahvki* – standardised suspended (ie, external) refuelling unit.)

Production land-based Su-27s did not receive IFR capability. Still, a single Su-27P (c/n 36911037820, f/n 37-20) was retrofitted with an IFR probe as tested on the T10U-2. Redesignated Su-27PD (D for *dozaprahvka* – refuelling) and coded 598 White, it was delivered to the *Ispytahteli* (Test pilots) display team operated by the Flight Research Institute (LII – *Lyotno-issledovatel'skiy institoot*) in Zhukovskiy near Moscow.

As already mentioned, the T10-24 was the first step in the Flanker's evolution towards ultra-manoeuvrability. The next step was taken in 1988 when the T10-26 development aircraft (26 Blue, c/n unknown, f/n 07-02), was converted into a testbed designated LL-UV (KS). This stood for *letayuschchaya laboratoriya s oopravlyayemym vektorom*

[*tyaghi*], *kroogloye soplo* – thrust-vectoring control (TVC) testbed, circular nozzle. (The Russian term *letayuschchaya laboratoriya* (lit. 'flying laboratory') is used indiscriminately and can denote any kind of testbed or research/survey aircraft.) One of the fighter's Lyul'ka AL-31F afterburning turbofans was fitted with an experimental axisymmetrical convergent-divergent nozzle which could be deflected up and down at certain angles.

Flight tests began in 1989 and quickly confirmed the advantages conferred by TVC. Compared to the standard Su-27, the T10-26 had better agility and the ability to maintain controlled flight at much lower speeds.

Since the best configuration of the fifth-generation fighter's vectoring nozzles was still undetermined at the time, Sukhoi engineers took TVC studies further with another testbed. This was converted from a pre-production KnAAPO-built Su-27UB coded 08 Blue (c/n unknown, f/n 02-02) in 1990 and bore the designation LL-UV (PS), which stands for *letayuschchaya laboratoriya s oopravlyayemym vektorom* [*tyaghi*], *ploskoye soplo* (TVC testbed, 'flat', ie, two-dimensional nozzle). A long boxy extension was grafted onto the port engine, protruding beyond the tail 'stinger'. It incorporated a 2-D nozzle which, as in the case of the T10-26, offered pitch-only thrust vectoring.

LII also undertook several test programmes with a Su-27 coded 05 Red (c/n 36911024205, f/n 24-05). The aircraft was part of the LMK-2405

active flight safety research complex (*lyotno-modeleeru-yuschchiy kompleks* – 'in-flight simulation complex') designed for developing flight safety procedures and control techniques for tomorrow's super-agile fighters. The complex included a ground processing unit which analysed the aircraft's trajectory and systems operation and formulated control algorithms.

05 Red featured an advanced digital FBW control system with a sidestick (the standard control stick was retained as a backup) and full-authority digital engine control (FADEC). Flight and systems data were fed to the ground in real time by an omnidirectional data link system with aerials aft of the cockpit and under the port air intake. Multi-faceted angle reflectors were fitted under the wingtips to give a better radar signature. For high-alpha/low-speed handling trials the aircraft could be equipped with spin recovery rockets on the outer wing pylons.

A number of other test and development versions of the Flanker was used to verify a wide range of new equipment, including new weapons systems. Numerous test programmes undertaken by Sukhoi, coupled with the company's wise economic policy (first and foremost regarding foreign sales), have enabled Sukhoi and their partners in research and manufacturing to develop a new product line – a range of advanced versions of the Su-27 family, many of which are second to none in performance and combat potential. These will be detailed below.

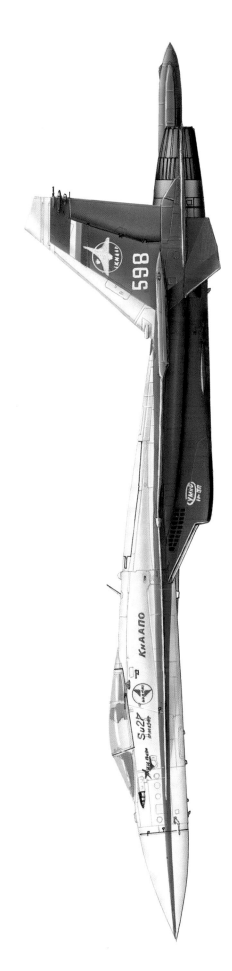

The Su-27PD (c/n 36811037820) of the *Ispytahteli* display team features a flight refuelling probe. This aircraft is flown by the team's leader Anatoliy N. Kvochur.

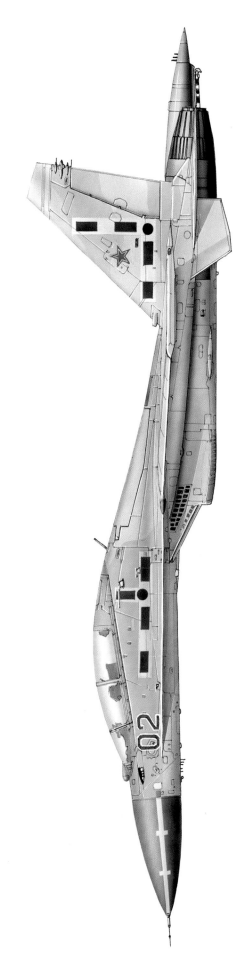

The T10U-2 development aircraft (f/n 02-01) in its latter days following installation of an arrestor hook.

The Su-27PD is fitted with a retractable refuelling probe (just visible ahead of the cockpit in this view).

The T10-26 CCV, alias LL-UV (KS).

Chapter 1

Building a Better Fighter

The excellent engineering level of the basic Su-27 enabled the Sukhoi OKB to develop a range of advanced tactical aircraft, starting in the mid-1980s. These aircraft (the above-mentioned 'Su-30 series') fill a variety of roles. We will deal with the single-seat air superiority fighters first, since this was the Flanker's original mission.

Chronologically the first of the 'Su-30 series' to fly – ahead of the aircraft which gave the series its name, – this fighter started life as the T10-M or Su-27M (*modern-izeerovannyy* – upgraded). Later the manufacturer's designation was changed to Su-35. The design effort led by chief project engineer Nikolay F. Nikitin was one of the greatest challenges for the OKB. Eventually, however, the Su-35 became one of its greatest engineering successes, epitomising the daring approach to upgrading when every component of an aircraft's combat efficiency – performance, avionics and armament – is improved.

The task facing the OKB was all the more daunting because the basic Su-27 was then one of the world's best fighters as it was; the whole affair looked rather like gilding the lily. Still, the engineers found ways of refining the Flanker's aerodynamics, as well as the armament and systems.

The most obvious new feature of the T10-M was the addition of canards which had been tested on the T10-24 control configured vehicle. They were relatively small, accounting for only 5% of the aircraft's lifting area. The canards made the aircraft more agile, especially at AoAs around 120°. This was a logical development of the LERXes – the heart of the vortex system accounting for the Su-27's unique agility. The canards directed the vortices in such a way as to delay airflow separation from the wings and horizontal tail. Besides increasing lift during sharp manoeuvres in a dogfight, this virtually eliminated high-alpha buffeting which caused control problems and made weapons aiming difficult on previous versions of the Su-27.

The canards were included into the FBW control system and could be deflected at

The first Su-27M prototype, the T10M-1, at the Sukhoi OKB's flight test facility in Zhukovskiy.

+10°... -50°, depending on the aircraft's AoA. Thus they acted almost as leading-edge slats (thanks to the airflow interaction between them and the wings), improving lift/drag ratio during manoeuvres and easing the bending loads on the wings and fuselage at the wing roots. It was this redistribution of aerodynamic loads that gave the T10-M a sizeable advantage over the production Su-27 (T10-S). The canards increased the aircraft's static instability 3 to 5 times and the critical AoA at which directional control was lost increased from 20° to 30°. (Speaking of which, the leading-edge flaps also helped a lot; at 30° alpha the rudders retained 50% of their efficiency at 0° alpha.) Besides, the canards also had a passive/active pitch damping function in turbulence (notably during ultra-low-level flight), giving the aircraft a smoother ride.

Thus, the chosen configuration (sometimes erroneously referred to as 'triplane configuration' in the popular press) and the shape of the LERXes improved high-alpha airflow, giving better pitch response and reducing aerodynamic loads at high AoAs. This allowed the T10-M to pull 10 Gs briefly without requiring structural reinforcement and hence incurring a weight penalty. Trim drag in supersonic cruise was also reduced.

In order to select the best camouflage for the Su-27M, the T10M-1 received this unusual scheme. The 'scars' on the wings are test equipment sensors sealed with a special compound.

The third prototype, T10M-3, in its original camouflage and with Sorbtsiya jammer pods on the wingtips.

The same aircraft following repaint in a splinter camouflage.

The Cobra and tailslide allowed Flanker pilots to redefine dogfight tactics. Instead of chasing the enemy in circles and 'snapping at his tail', the pilot could pitch up on the first turn, rotating the aircraft through 120° in 1.5 seconds to 'look over his shoulder'. The radar and infra-red search & track unit/laser range-finder (IRST/LR) would acquire the target immediately and automatically trigger the launch of two missiles. The tailslide, on the other hand, is a good defensive tactic. Realising the enemy is on his tail, the pilot of the T10-M can do a tailslide, decelerating rapidly. This causes the attacker to lose radar lock-on and overshoot – and then the tables are turned: the hunter becomes prey.

Apart from the canards, the Su-27M (T10-M) differed from the standard Su-27 (T10-S) in a number of respects. First, the standard AL-31F engines rated at 12,500 kgp (27,557 lb st) in full afterburner were replaced by experimental AL-31FMs uprated to 12,800 kgp (28,218 lb st). (Once again, the M stands for *modernizeerovannyy* – upgraded.)

Second, for better directional stability (to compensate for the higher gross weight) the T10-M had taller vertical tails of increased area and thickness with horizontally cropped tips; they were made of carbonfibre reinforced plastic (CFRP) and incorporated integral fuel tanks. Third, the weapons control system (WCS) was new, comprising a new powerful multi-mode fire control radar. This necessitated the use of a recontoured radome which was of true ogival shape (unlike the radomes of standard single- and two-seat Flankers which had double curvature) and was not tipped with a pitot.

Moreover, the aircraft was virtually spin-proof. If it did flip into a spin due to battle damage, the control system would initiate recovery automatically with minimum loss of altitude. The T10-M was the world's first fighter to incorporate the automatic spin prevention/recovery feature; this necessitated changes to the FBW control system software. The 1995 landing accident in which the Lockheed Martin/Boeing YF-22 prototype was written off had been caused by problems with the FBW controls; the fact that Soviet engineers had designed that problem out of the T10-M thirteen years earlier says a lot for

the technological lead of the Russian control systems design school.

The measures described above gave the T10-M a lift/drag ratio of 2 in sustained subsonic flight at AoAs around 30°. The aircraft became much easier to fly during such complex dogfight manoeuvres as the Pugachov Cobra (a pitch-up beyond 90° to the direction of flight) executed in straight and level flight, vertical climb or during turns. (The latter kind is also known as the Cobra Turn or 'hook', ie, swinging blow.) In all cases the fighter reached AoAs right up to 120° without showing any tendency to stall or spin.

Fourth, a new radar homing and warning system (RHAWS) was installed. Fifth, the aircraft had a retractable refuelling probe offset to port. Finally, two additional pylons were fitted under the inner wings, increasing the number of hardpoints to 12 and the ordnance load to 8,000 kg (17,636 lb).

The aircraft was capable of attacking enemy aircraft at long range ('first sight, first shot, first kill' capability), destroying ground targets at up to 120 km (66 nm) range, conduct group operations against aerial and ground targets with automatic target distribution within the group. The T10-M's IFR capability also enabled it to perform combat air patrol (CAP) and long-range escort duties.

Advanced features enhancing the fighter's combat potential included automation of all flight and weapons delivery modes (including automatic terrain following), a capable electronic countermeasures (ECM) suite, automatic systems status monitoring right down to line replaceable units (LRUs), the use of avionics with artificial intelligence, as well as duplication and high ECM resistance of all data processing systems.

The improved digital weapons control system (designated RLSU-27M for *rahdiolokatseeonnaya sistems oopravleniya* – 'radar control system'), enabled the fighter to detect and destroy all types of aerial targets, including 'stealthy' aircraft and cruise missiles with a small radar cross-section (RCS). It was built around the N-011 fire control radar developed by MNIIP (*Moskovskiy naoochno-issledovatel'skiy instituut preeborostroyeniya* – Moscow Research Institute of Instrument Engineering named after Viktor V. Tikhomeerov), aka NPO Vega-M, under chief project engineer T. O. Bekirbayev. This coherent pulse-Doppler radar is virtually jamproof and can track 15 aerial targets while guiding AAMs to six priority threats. (The original specification called for 20 targets and eight priority threats, but this goal was not achieved until much later.) It also has ground mapping functions for navigation, detection of moving ground targets and 'obstacle jumping' during ultra-low-level flight.

The N-011 has a flat-plate scanner. The beam is scanned mechanically in azimuth and electronically in elevation; the field of view is 90° both in azimuth and in elevation. Detection range for a typical fighter-type target with an RCS of 3 m² (32.25 sq. ft) is 80 to 100 km (44 to 55 nm). On the down side, the new radar is rather heavier than the Flanker-B/C's N-001 Mech (Sword). Hence the standard nose landing gear unit with a single 680x260 mm (26.7x10.2 in.) wheel and wraparound mudguard had to be replaced by a reinforced unit with twin 620x180 mm (24.4x7.08 in.) wheels and a redesigned mudguard to absorb the extra weight.

The T10-M was to be equipped with a MNIIP N-012 rear warning radar in a modified fat tail 'stinger' – a world's first among fighters. This feature would make the fighter virtually immune against attacks from behind. This required the brake parachute container to be moved forward and redesigned (it popped up like a jack-in-the-box).

The fire control radar was linked to a new optoelectronic targeting system. The latter included an IRST, a laser rangefinder and a helmet-mounted sight. The IRST/LR's field of view was 120° in azimuth and +60°/-12° in elevation.

As already mentioned, the T10-M had 12 hardpoints but the number of external stores could be increased by using multiple ejector racks (MERs). Weapons used in the air superiority role included R-73E (NATO AA-11 *Archer*) short-range AAMs with an all-aspect passive IR seeker head, R-27R1/R-27RE1 (AA-10 *Alamo*) medium-range semi-active radar homing (SARH) missiles, R-27T1/R-27TE1 medium-range passive IR-homing AAMs and R-77 (AA-12 *Adder*), aka RVV-AE (*raketa 'vozdookh-vozdookh', aktivnaya, eksportnaya* – air-to-air missile, active [radar homing], export version), medium-range active radar-homing AAMs. All of these

The T10M-3 entered flight test on 1st April 1992 (that was *not* meant as an April Fool's Day joke).

The Su-27M could carry a wide range of weapons. Here, the T10M-3 carries a Kh-31P anti-radiation missile under the port wing.

weapons have been developed by the Vympel (Pennant) OKB. (With the R-27, the R suffix denotes *rahdiolokatseeonnaya [golovka sahmonavedeniya]* – radar homing, T stands for *teplovaya [golovka sahmonave-deniya]* – IR homing, while E means [*povyshennaya*] *energiya* – 'high energy', ie, longer-burn rocket motor.)

In the strike role the aircraft was armed with Vympel Kh-29T (TV-guided) and Kh-29L (laser-guided) air-to-ground missiles (AS-14 Kedge); Kh-59M Ovod-M (Gadfly-M/AS-18 Kazoo) TV-guided tactical cruise missiles developed by MKB Raduga (Rainbow, pronounced *rahdooga*); Kh-31A anti-shipping missiles and Kh-31P anti-radiation missiles (AS-17 Krypton) developed by NPO Zvezda (Star, pronounced *zvezdah*). Additionally, 500-kg (1,102-lb) KAB-500Kr and 1,500-kg (3,306-lb) KAB-1500L guided bombs could be carried. (KAB = *korrekteerooyemaya aviabomba* – guided bomb. The KAB-500Kr is TV-guided and the KAB-1500L is laser-guided.) Other stores included 100/250/500-kg (220/551/1,102-lb) free-fall bombs, cluster bombs/submunitions dispensers (including parachute-retarded bomblets for low-level sorties) and napalm tanks. The total number of weapons configurations exceeded 70; other weapons were to be integrated later on.

In designing the T10-M Sukhoi paid special attention to improving working conditions for the pilot. As mentioned earlier, all flight and combat modes were automated as much as possible. For the first time on a Soviet fighter, the aircraft had an electronic flight instrumentation system (EFIS) or 'glass cockpit' featuring colour liquid-crystal multi-function displays (MFDs). The avionics suite was built around a high-speed processor which took care of various tasks – from mission

plan entry to weapons control, utilising typical combat scenarios stored in its memory to give the required information and 'hints' to the pilot. The MFDs helped to reduce pilot workload, providing him with all the controls he needed at any one time in a convenient arrangement.

The incline of the K-36DM ejection seat was increased to 30°, easing the effect of high G loads on the pilot. The avionics suite's built-in test equipment (BITE) minimised mission preparation time and reduced the need for ground support equipment, making the aircraft easier to operate. The capacity of the oxygen system was increased as compared to the Su-27; food and water containers were provided for long sorties, as was a waste disposal device.

All ten prototypes, designated T10M-1 through T10M-10 and coded 701 through 710, were built by KnAAPO but not all of them were new-build aircraft. Wearing the low-visibility tactical code 701 Black outline, the first prototype, was converted from a standard T10-S built in 1986 (c/n 36911016202; the f/n has been reported as 16-40). It made its first post-conversion flight on 28th June 1988 at the hands of Sukhoi chief test pilot Oleg G. Tsoi. In 1990 the aircraft was displayed to top-ranking Soviet Ministry of Defence officials at Kubinka AB some 65 km (40 miles) west of Moscow.

(**Note:** Su-27s built by KnAAPO have 11-digit c/ns – eg, 36911024205. The meaning is apparently as follows. The first three digits are a code for the factory (later changed to 490 and still later to 798 in order to confuse spies, giving the impression that different factories were involved). The next three digits denote the version: 110 (ie, version 1 of the T-10) = Su-27 Flanker-B, 210 = Su-27UB

Flanker-C, 510 = Su-27K Flanker-D, 710 = Su-27M. The version designators were not allocated consecutively – probably again for security reasons. The remaining digits were originally thought to denote the production batch, the team of workers assembling the specific aircraft and the number of the aircraft in the batch, as had been the case with the Su-17/-22 *Fitter-B et seq.* also built by KnAAPO (i.e., Batch 24, assembled by team 2, fifth aircraft in the batch). Recently, however, some aircraft have been reported with fuselage numbers which do not match the last five of the c/n. On KnAAPO-built aircraft the c/n is normally stencilled in the port main-wheel well.

Also note that three-digit tactical codes were rare in the Soviet Air Force and usually allocated to development aircraft only, often tying in with the aircaft's c/n, f/n or manufacturer's designation. This does not apply to some SovAF transport aircraft which were previously quasi-civilian; these had tactical codes matching the last three digits of the former civil registration.)

Unlike most of the Su-27M prototypes, the T10M-1 had standard (ie, short) Flanker-B vertical tails with raked dielectric fin caps and *sans* integral tanks. The new WCS was not yet fitted (the aircraft was intended for handling tests), hence the T10M-1 retained the standard single-wheel nose gear unit and the usual ten weapons hardpoints. There was no IFR probe and the IRST/LR 'ball' ahead of the windscreen was replaced with a metal fairing.

Test equipment sensors were attached to the wing upper surface and the starboard fin to measure structural loads; the sensors and their wiring were protected by a sealing compound, resulting in some strange-looking

The T10M-9 in its current desert camouflage caught on LII's runway in Zhukovskiy.

'scars' on the airframe. This technique of attaching test equipment sensors was developed in the Soviet Union. More sensors were apparently mounted on the outer faces of the engine nacelles just aft of the intakes, as indicated by some non-standard metal plates where ECM antennas are usually installed on the standard Su-27.

The fighter sported an unusual five-tone grey colour scheme, the colours fanning out from the nose on both upper and lower surfaces, growing darker towards the tail. This experimental paint job was designed to select the most effective camouflage; apparently the T10M-1 was photographed from the ground and from high-flying aircraft to see how the colours blended with the surroundings. The national insignia were presented in an unusual low-visibility style, consisting of only a red outline.

The second prototype (T10M-2, coded 702) – also a converted Flanker-B – joined the test programme in January 1989. The next aircraft, T10M-3 (703 Blue outline, c/n 79871010102), took off on 1st April 1992. This was the first Su-27M (Su-35) to be built as such; it was also the first example to have the intended tall square-tipped fins, twin-wheel nose gear and flight refuelling capability. (As already mentioned, the '710' in the c/n

The T10M-9 makes a demonstration flight with a full complement of dummy missiles.

An interesting view of both splinter-camouflaged Su-27Ms (the T10M-3 and T10M-9) taking off.

The T10M-9 on landing.

This rare shot by the well-known aviation photographer Katsuhiko Tokunaga shows two Su-27Ms during a test flight. The T10M-9 pulls away from the T10M-3 carrying a guided bomb, among other things.

probably denotes 'version 7 of the T-10'. This probably explains why the tactical codes of the Su-27M (Su-35) prototypes begin with a 7.)

The new fighter was unveiled under the official designation Su-27M on 13th February 1992 when the leaders of the CIS republics inspected the sixth prototype, T10M-6 (706 Blue outline), at Machoolischchi AB near Minsk. Soon afterwards, in the summer of 1992, the T10M-7 (707 Blue outline) was demonstrated to Russian Air Force C-in-C Col Gen Pyotr S. Deynekin and the press at the Soviet Air Force Research Institute named after Valeriy P. Chkalov (NII VVS – *Naoochno-issledovatel'skiy institoot Voyenno-vozdooshnykh sil*; now the 929th GLITs – *Gosoodahrstvennyy lyotno-ispytahtel'nyy tsentr*, State Flight Test Centre). These aircraft wore standard Su-27 colours, as did most of the other prototypes, including the T10M-8 (708 Blue) and the T10M-10 (710 Blue, c/n 79871011002).

The Su-27Ms had detail differences. For example, the first, second, sixth and seventh development aircraft were converted Su-27s; hence they had standard short vertical tails, standard tail 'stingers' and single-wheel nose gear units, suggesting that the N-011 radar was not fitted to these aircraft. The other six prototypes (703 through 705 and 708 through 710) had twin-wheel nose gear units and tall CFRP fins featuring squared-off tips and integral tanks. Additionally, the new-build Su-27Ms featured bigger fuel tanks in the wing torsion box (these were limited by rib No. 13 instead of rib No. 9 as on the Flanker-B/C). As a result, the internal fuel load was increased by 850 kg (1,874 lb) to 10,250 kg (22,597 lb).

The short-tailed T10M-1, T10M-6 and T10M-7 were used by NII VVS in a large-scale test programme and flown by Air Force pilots, operating from Akhtoobinsk near Saratov on the Volga River in southern Russia. Conversely, the third, ninth and tenth aircraft were based in Zhukovskiy most of the time and flown mostly by Sukhoi test pilots.

Soon after the Su-27M's Machoolischchi debut the Powers That Be decided to show the new fighter to the outside world. By then the aircraft had been redesignated Su-35 to emphasise how different it was from the production Su-27. Thus the T10M-3 was displayed statically at the Farnborough International '92 airshow. Besides being an airshow debutante, the Su-35 raised a few eyebrows by appearing with a Ferranti thermal imaging and airborne laser device (TIALD); this was probably the first time a Russian combat aircraft came with Western avionics.

At FI'92 the T10M-3 still wore the standard two-tone blue camouflage applied to Soviet Air Force Su-27s. The following year, however, it was repainted in a striking three-tone disruptive camouflage with two vivid

The T10M-10, the final Su-27M prototype, at LII's airfield in Zhukovskiy.

The T10M-10 lines up for take-off.

shades of blue and light grey. The ninth prototype aircraft, T10M-9 (709 Blue, c/n 79871011001), also originally painted in standard blue camouflage, later received a similar splinter scheme but in 'tropical' shades of tan, leaf green and chocolate brown (and became 709 Black outline). These two aircraft were intended for demonstration work abroad, hence the odd paint jobs.

In 1993 the T10M-3 appeared at the IDEX'93 defence fair in Dubai its new disruptive colour scheme (though the desert-camouflaged T10M-9 would have been more appropriate at that particular show). Accompanied by the Su-30MK prototype (603 Black outline), the Su-35 arrived in Dubai under its own power (not in the belly of an airlifter). The Su-30MK (see next chapter) put on a lively aerobatics display including some elements that could give the pilot a decisive advantage in a dogfight – the Flanker's trademark Pugachov Cobra and the unfamiliar Cobra Turn.

The cockpit of the T10M-10 features three MFDs.

17

One of the three production Su-35s on display at the Russian Air Force's 929th State Flight Test Centre (GLITs) in Akhtoobinsk.

The cherry on the cake was a session of mock combat between the Su-30MK and the Su-35; it was enough to draw the spectators out of the air-conditioned pavilions and chalets into the searing heat (the ambient temperature in Dubai was 40°C/104°F). Sukhoi OKB test pilot Viktor G. Pugachov who was flying the Su-35 would pull his famous Cobra, causing the two-seater to overshoot. The Su-30MK then rolled right and the fighters would start chasing each other's tails, trying to get into position to fire. Halfway through the turn Pugachov snapped his fighter up into the Cobra Turn, got a lock-on, and the pursuer was toast – or so it would be in real combat.

During the Cobra Turn the Su-35 decelerated quickly from 460 km/h (255 kts) to 250 km/h (138 kts), pulling 9 Gs with 90° bank.

Still, the aircraft showed no tendency to stall or lose control because of airflow separation. During the Cobra manoeuvre the aircraft gained some 30 m (98 ft) of altitude, allowing the pilot to put the nose down in order to accelerate.

For safety's sake the pilots started practising the Cobra Turn at about 11,000 m (36,089 ft), gradually decreasing altitude and speed. Soon they had no problems performing the manoeuvre at 5,000 m (16,404 ft). Since the Cobra Turn results in a loss of speed, the pilot has to begin a shallow dive in order to regain speed quickly after recovery.

In May-June 1993 Russian and foreign aviation experts had the chance to see Viktor Pugachov perform the Cobra Turn on the third prototype Su-35 carrying a full load of 12 AAMs. A year later spectators at ILA'94

were treated to the same experience. The Su-35 became a regular participant at all major airshows, including MAKS-93 (31st August to 5th September 1993), the 41st Paris Air Show, where it had the exhibit code 350, and MAKS-95 (22nd-27th August 1995). At MAKS-99 (17th-22nd August 1999) the T10M-9 was displayed with an impressive weapons array including, for the first time, a K310MA-03 Yakhont (Emerald) anti-shipping missile developed by the Reutov-based NPO Mashinostroyeniya.

Unfortunately, despite the promise it held, the T10-M did not reach operational status. At one time the Republic of Korea Air Force (ROKAF) expressed an interest in the Su-35 but did not follow up with an order. As for the home market, the Russian Air Force ordered a small batch of Su-27Ms for evaluation pur-

Left, an overall view of the AL-31FP engine and, right, its axisymmetrical vectoring nozzle.

The thrust-vectoring T10M-11 was a joint effort of the Sukhoi OKB, NPO Saturn and several other research and development establishments.

poses when the T10-M was close to completing its State acceptance (ie certification) trials. (The Russian military do not use the Su-35 designation.)

Low-rate initial production began in the mid-1990s and the first aircraft were due for delivery to the 234th *Proskoorovskiy* GvIAP (*Gvardeyskiy istrebitel'nyy aviapolk* – Guards fighter regiment) at Kubinka AB as early as 1995. (The honorary appellation *Proskoorovskiy* marks the unit's valour in liberating the town of Proskoorovo during the Second World War.) Eventually, however, the unit never got them. Three production Su-27Ms completed in 1996 (coded 86 Red, 87 Red and 88 Red) and wearing an unusual lurid turquoise camouflage were delivered to the 929th GLITs in Akhtoobinsk for trials, and there they remain as of this writing. In the meantime, even more sophisticated versions of the Flanker (and low-cost upgrade programmes) have appeared. That said, the chance of the Su-27M ever entering quantity production and service is very small indeed.

Su-27M '87 Red' was on display during the festivities marking the 70th anniversary of NII VVS in 1996. Another example, 88 Red, was on show at a similar event in late 2000 on occasion of the Centre's 75th anniversary. Unfortunately, no-one obtained their c/ns.

In the course of its flight tests the T10-M (Su-35) had performed manoeuvres involving high AoAs and airspeeds close to zero. The Pugachov Cobra, Cobra Turn and tailslide could be used in air-to-air combat; however, active control in these flight modes was virtually impossible because the control surfaces

were inefficient at low airspeeds. The pilot could not control the aircraft's pitch/roll rate or maintain high alpha, which left him very little time to get a target lock-on and fire a missile.

Thrust-vectoring control (TVC) was the solution. It was the key to ultra-manoeuvrability which enabled the fighter to remain in the zero-speed/high-alpha mode for three or four seconds (ie, long enough to get a lock-on and fire a missile) or quickly recover from this mode.

The Sukhoi OKB began initial TVC studies as early as 1983. The Western press then described two-dimensional vectoring nozzles as the best option; however, General Designer (the official title of Soviet/Russian OKB heads) Mikhail P. Simonov insisted on using axisymmetrical vectoring nozzles.

At Sukhoi's request SibNIA conducted a series of experiments with such nozzles – using scale models, not real engines, since the objective was to test nozzle operation. (It should be noted that the institute had studied 2-D vectoring nozzles as well.) By 1985 Sukhoi engineers had a clear picture of the forces generated by movable nozzles. Work on thrust-vectoring engines and aircraft powered by such engines could now begin. Thus, by the mid-80s the Soviet Union had the know-how to create a TVC fighter.

Actual work on an upgraded version of the T10-M with thrust-vectoring engines began in 1988. The main reason behind it was the need to enhance the Flanker family's manoeuvrability both at high speeds with high G forces and at low speeds which were unthinkable for a jet fighter until then. All the

experience accumulated with the Su-27/Su-35 and the latest technology were brought into play.

In 1988 and 1990 Sukhoi began a series of tests with the LL-UV (KS) and LL-UV (PS) testbeds described earlier. On these aircraft the vectoring nozzle could only move up and down. The results were generally encouraging and work on a TVC version of the T10-M proceeded apace.

The first genuinely thrust-vectoring Flanker was the eleventh prototype Su-35 (T10M-11). The aircraft was developed as a joint effort by Sukhoi, NPO Lyul'ka-Saturn and several other R&D establishments and companies, including the French avionics house Sextant Avionique. The new AL-31FU engine (U = *oopravlyayemoye soplo* – 'controlled' (ie, movable) nozzle) uprated to 12,800 kgp (28,218 lb st) in full afterburner was selected to power the fighter. A curious feature of the AL-31FU was that the axisymmetrical nozzle was vectored by tilting a hinged circular frame to which the nozzle petals were attached, rather than by moving the petals proper.

Like all previous T10-M prototypes and the initial production Su-27Ms, the T10M-11 was built by KnAAPO. The airframe was completed in early 1995 but the intended AL-31FU engines had not been flight-cleared yet. Hence AL-31FPs (P = *povorotnoye soplo* – movable nozzle) were temporarily fitted. The AL-31FP was, in effect, a standard 12,500-kgp (27,557-lb st) AL-31F fitted with the AL-100 vectoring nozzle of the AL-31FU. Of course, the less powerful engines would

19

This view of the T10M-11 shows to advantage the movable nozzles of the AL-31FP engines which 'bleed' down after engine shutdown.

give a reduction in performance but, at any rate, this stopgap measure allowed the T10M-11 to be delivered to Sukhoi's experimental shop so that ground tests could begin before the end of the year.

Unlike production Su-27s which had an analogue FBW control system, the T10M-11 featured digital FBW controls. The system had a quadruplex pitch control circuit and triplex yaw and roll control circuits; all control system computers operated in parallel for added reliability.

The automatic flight control system governed the vectoring nozzles as well as the control surfaces. It limited G loads automatically to suit the aircraft's all-up weight and flight mode. This was a safety measure to prevent the airframe from being overstressed. As on the Su-35, an automatic spin recovery function was provided; thus, the pilot could concentrate wholly on doing his job without having to worry about G loads and AoAs, or about airspeed getting out of hand in the heat of the battle.

The cockpit was equipped a limited-travol side-stick (which, like the digital FBW control system, had been put through its paces on the abovementioned LMK-2405 CCV) and pressure-sensing throttles – 'power-by-wire'. These features made for more precise flying and enhanced flight safety, eliminating the risk of the pilot inadvertently moving the stick or throttles as he should not during high-G manoeuvres. The integrated full authority digital engine control (FADEC) system with automatic thrust vector control made the T10M-11 extremely agile at high alpha and ultra-low speeds.

Other changes in the cockpit included four large colour liquid-crystal displays (LCDs) sup-plied by Sextant Avionique; these had better backlight protection than cathode-ray tubes (CRTs). The LCDs were arranged in T fashion and comprised a multi-function air data/navigation display, a tactical situation display, a systems status screen and a weapons/systems selection display. All four LCDs were interchangeable and the pilot could select the required information on any of them. A wide-angle multi-function head-up display (HUD) was also fitted. The increased incline of the ejection seat (30°) enabled the pilot to absorb higher G loads while remaining fully in control; this allowed him to use the aircraft's capabilities to the full, increasing the chances of mission success.

The mission avionics were also improved. The T10M-11 was to feature an upgraded NIIP N-011M Bars (Leopard) coherent pulse-Doppler fire control radar and the N-012 rear-warning radar. The N-011M was developed for the latest members of the 'Su-30 series' – the Su-37, Su-30MKI and Su-35UB (the latter two are described in the next chapter). It had a fixed phased array; the beam was scanned electronically through ±90° in azimuth and ±55° in elevation. The radar could track up to 20 aerial targets with a 3-m² (32.25-sq. ft) RCS at 140 to 160 km (77 to 88 nm), guiding AAMs to eight priority threats. Ground targets with a 3,000-m² (32,258-sq. ft) RCS, such as surface ships, could be detected at 130 to 170 km (72 to 94 nm).The N-012 had a 120° field of view in both azimuth and elevation, detecting a fighter-type target at 30 to 50 km (16 to 27 nm).

The electronic support measures (ESM) suite was upgraded considerably, featuring a new-generation signals intelligence (SIGINT) pack, an infra-red missile warning system (MWS), a RHAWS, active radar and laser jammers, and chaff/flare dispensers. The communications suite included HF and VHF radios, secure data link and satellite communications equipment. The new avionics and equipment consumed more electric and hydraulic power, requiring the provision of more powerful generators and pumps.

Painted in a tan/dark earth disruptive camouflage and initially coded 711 Blue, the T10M-11 made its first flight on 2nd April 1996 at the hands of Yevgeniy I. Frolov (Hero of Russia). Igor' V. Votintsev, another Sukhoi OKB test pilot, joined the test programme soon afterwards. By 14 June Frolov and Votintsev had made 12 flights in the T10M-11 between them.

In the spring of 1996 the T10M-11 was unveiled for industry experts and the press in Zhukovskiy. The scenario was repeated – the aircraft received a new official designation, Su-37, because of the major changes to the powerplant and avionics.

Piloted by Yevgeniy Frolov, the Su-37 stole the show at Farnborough International '96 in September – and with good reason, too. With all control surfaces and the vectoring nozzles moving in concert, the aircraft is capable of pitching up through 180° (!) and staying in this tail-first position long enough to fire a missile at a pursuing enemy fighter. This spectacular manoeuvre has been called the Super Cobra – or, as Frolov calls it, the Stop Cobra. The lack of limits on AoA and pitch rate has made it possible to use the sizeable additional lift generated by the unstable airflow in certain attitudes.

The Super Cobra logically evolved into a 360° somersault that has become known as the Frolov Chakra – another unique manoeuvre that invariably leaves the audience gaping. Other manoeuvres performed by the Su-37 include a high-speed yo-yo executed in less than ten seconds, a stall turn in a vertical climb, Cobra manoeuvres with AoAs of 150 to 180° (with an attitude hold of three or four seconds), a tailslide transforming into a wingover and so on. This ultra-manoeuvrability is an invaluable asset in a dogfight, especially if the opponent is a modern high-tech fighter.

The Su-37 has all the strengths of its precursor, the Su-35 – agility, 'first sight, first shot, first kill' capability against enemy aircraft (including stealthy ones), duplicated and jamproof targeting and data processing systems, the ability to destroy ground targets while staying out of range of enemy air defences, high ECM capability, automation of all flight modes, including terrain following and group action. It just takes them one step further.

Of course, everything comes at a price. On internal fuel only the Su-37 has shorter range than the Su-27 (3,880 km/2,155 nm) because of the added weight of the new avionics. However, with aerial refuelling capability this is clearly not a problem.

In 1997 Sukhoi entered the Su-37 in the exhibit list of the 42nd Paris Air Show at Le Bourget. However, the road to Paris turned out to be long and arduous. The busy flight test programme and bureaucratic snags conspired against the Su-37, and the Russian MoD did not authorise the aircraft to be demonstrated at Le Bourget – regardless of the fact that it had been displayed in the West a year before! Bureaucratic nonsense is the same in every part of the world.

Test pilot Yevgeniy Frolov, who arrived in Paris in an airliner instead of the Su-37, did not let things slide. He was ready to address just about anyone in high places to get permission for the Su-37 to go to Le Bourget. Help often comes when you least expect it. One meeting with Yakov Urinson, who was then Russian Vice Prime Minister and Minister of Economics (and chairman of the Russian delegation at the show), and the Russian ambassador in France Mr. Ryzhov was all it took. The state machinery was set in motion; somebody in the MoD apparently got a dressing-down and the go-ahead was received within 24 hours, with all papers duly signed.

The aircraft arrived in Paris on 19th June, the closing day of the airshow, wearing the exhibit code 344; the tactical code had by then changed from 711 Blue to 711 White. News of the fighter's impending arrival spread quickly, and many of the industry delegations at Le Bourget delayed their departure just to have a look at the Su-37 which they had by then given up as a 'no-show'. However, the flight display was marred by an incident. The first three demo flights went OK but on the fourth flight the landing gear would

The fat tail 'stinger of the Su-37 was to house an N-012 rear warning radar (apparently not yet fitted).

not retract. Frolov did a Cobra and landed hastily, cutting the display short. It was quickly established that someone had moved the emergency extension handle, disabling gear retraction. A little thing like this was of course fixed immediately, and 711 White performed another display routine flawlessly. The big question was *who* had moved the confounded handle, and *why?*

Soon afterwards the aircraft participated in the MAKS-97 airshow (19th-24th August), making mostly demo flights and appearing in the static park on the last-but-one day only. This time Sukhoi representatives on site did their utmost to prevent anyone from getting too close to the fighter, probably fearing more damage to the aircraft. (And with good reason, too – the spectators can go a bit wild sometimes.) At the IDEX'97 trade fair in Dubai and the FIDAE'98 airshow in Santiago de Chile (the latter event started on 23rd March 1998) the T10M-11 was somewhat surprisingly demonstrated under a new designation, Su-37MR; no one seems to know what the R stands for! (The most common use of theis suffix is to denote [*samolyot-*] *razvedchik* –reconnaissance aircraft; possibly the idea was that the Su-37 would carry podded ELINT equipment and/or cameras.)

Test and demonstration flights have shown the AL-31FP's excellent resistance to surge, even when the aircraft literally travels tail first. This is doubtlessly a major achievement of NPO Lyul'ka-Saturn currently led by A. M. Lyul'ka's successor, General Designer Viktor Mikhailovich Chepkin.

The AL-31FP benefited from experience gained with the AL-31F in 1979-85, as well as twelve years of R&D work on the AL-41F thrust-vectoring afterburning turbofan devel-

oped for fifth-generation tactical aircraft. It employed Lyul'ka-Saturn's proprietary knowledge in such problem areas as sealing the joint between the engine casing and the movable nozzle to prevent seepage of hot gases, cooling the nozzle in full afterburner at maximum deflection and ensuring high surge resistance during violent manoeuvres. The AL-31FP's axisymmetrical nozzle is attached to an annular frame powered by two pairs of hydraulic rams, tilting vertically through ±15°. The frame is made of steel on prototype engines, but titanium will be used on production engines to save weight. Also, the nozzle tilting mechanism is hydraulically-actuated on prototype engines but will be powered by the fuel system on production engines to improve survivability.

Sealing the casing/nozzle joint effectively was perhaps the biggest challenge, since seepage of exhaust gases with a temperature around 2,000°C (3,632°F) and a pressure around 15 kg/cm^2 (214 psi) was guaranteed to cause a fire. Another major task solved by the engineers was complete nozzle control automation, as the pilot should not have to work separate TVC levers or switches. The nozzle is controlled by digital computers forming part of the FBW control system; the pilot simply works the stick and pedals, and the computers take care of the rest. Another ingenious feature of the AL-31FP is the monocrystalline turbine blades designed for very high operational loads.

The AL-31FP runs stably during inlet surge at up to Mach 2.0, as well as during 'classic', inverted and flat spins. This contributes immensely to the Su-37's unique agility, enabling it to travel briefly tail-first at 200 km/h (111 kts) during the Frolov Chakra.

A fine study of the T10M-11 (Su-37) during a test flight.

The engine is tough and virtually impervious to surge, and that means reliability. NPO Lyul'ka-Saturn has developed a series of modifications reducing the engine's IR signature at full military power, and these are offered as a customer option.

The AL-31FP's time until the first overhaul was originally 1,000 hours; the AL-100 nozzle's service life was 250 hours, though this was to be doubled when the engine completed its bench test programme. The engine's dry weight is 1,570 kg (3,461 lb); minimum cruise specific fuel consumption (SFC) is 0.677 kg/kgp.hr (lb/lb st.hr) and weight-to-thrust ratio is 0.115. The AL-31FP is 4.99 m (16 ft 4.45 in.) long and has an inlet diameter of 0.91 m (2 ft 11.82 in.), though some sources state 0.932 m (3 ft 0.64 in.); maximum diameter is 1.28 m (4 ft 2.39 in.).

However, it is the uprated AL-31FU that is scheduled to enter production at the Ufa engine factory in Bashkiria. This engine was unveiled at the '**Dvee**gatelestro**yen***iye*-96' (Engine Design '96) trade exhibition in Moscow. The AL-31FU has a maximum afterburner rating of 14,000 to 14,500 kgp (30,864 to 31,966 lb st) and runs more stably in minimum-speed flight. The engine will be manufactured in standard and tropicalized versions (the latter is intended for SE Asia and has improved corrosion protection).

The AL-31F-powered Su-27 and AL-31FM-powered Su-35 can do things other fighters cannot – for instance, formate with a helicopter flying at 200 km/h (111 kts), but the production Su-37 will do better still. The 28,000-kgp (61,728-lb st) aggregate thrust of two AL-31FUs will enable the 25,000-kg (55,114-lb) aircraft to literally stand still on its tail in the air, manoeuvring at speeds when conventional control surfaces are no longer effective.

The uniquely manoeuvrable multi-role Su-37 was just another logical step in the Sukhoi OKB's efforts to create a family of Generation 4+ and fifth-generation tactical aircraft based on the Su-27. Experts predicted that by 2020 these aircraft would be selling like hotcakes. At present, however, the Su-37's trials programme has virtually ground to a halt – mainly due to lack of customer interest for single-seaters. Foreign customers for the 'Su-30 series' – primarily the Indian Air Force and the Chinese People's Liberation Army Air Force (PLAAF) – prefer the two-seat Su-30MK which comes in customised versions. In the case of these two nations, it is the Su-30MKI (with TVC and canards) and the Su-30MKK (without TVC and canards) respectively.

Unlike the preceding versions of the Flanker family, the Su-27M (Su-35) and the Su-37 did not receive NATO reporting names (normally they would have been the Flanker-E and perhaps Flanker-F). This is mainly due to the new Soviet policy of openness; there was little point in inventing reporting names when the true designations were known.

From the outset the Su-27 had considerable export potential. Still, for various reasons – mainly political ones – exports of new Flankers were limited to India, China and Vietnam. (Su-27 sales to Yemen and Ethiopia in the late 1990s can be disregarded, as these were second-hand aircraft, not new.)

The export version of the Su-27 (T10-S) for China and Vietnam was designated Su-27SK. S means *sereeynyy* (production, used attributively) while K stands for *kommehrcheskiy* ('commercial', ie, downgraded 'customer version'). This letter was habitually used by Sukhoi for export versions since the early 1980s (cf. Su-24MK *Fencer-D*, Su-25K/Su-25UBK *Frogfoot-A/B*); the SK suffix was chosen to avoid confusion with the naval Su-27K described later in this book.

The Su-27SK differed from Soviet Air Force Su-27s and Air Defence Force Su-27Ps in having a reinforced landing gear, a MTOW increased to 33,000 kg (72,751 lb) and slightly downgraded avionics, with foreign avionics as a customer option.

Like the standard Su-27, the export version had ten hardpoints and, like Soviet Air Force Flanker-Bs, air-to-ground capability; its weapons range included AAMs, free-fall bombs, unguided rockets and submunitions dispensers. The maximum ordnance load was 6,000 kg (13,227 lb).

The Su-30KI taxies out for a demonstration flight on 19th August 1999 during the MAKS-99 airshow in Zhukovskiy.

The Su-30KI wore this unusual three-tone grey/black 'splatter camouflage'. Note the vertical stripes on the radome, which are probably phototheodolite calibration markings, and the 'Chinese-style' colouring of the radome.

The Su-30KI elegantly displays its upper surface as it makes a turn during a demo flight at MAKS-99.

Test pilot Viktor G. Pugachov takes off in the Su-30KI.

Top view of the T10M-1 (c/n 36911016202).

One of the three production Su-35 fighters.

The T10M-11 (Su-37) development aircraft.

The Su-30KI development aircraft (c/n 36911040102).

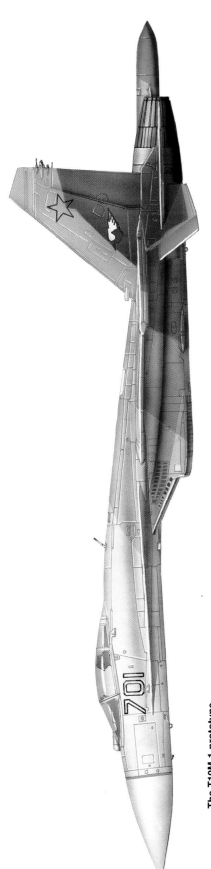

The T10M-1 prototype.

The third prototype Su-27M (T10M-3) with Sorbtsiya ECM pods at the wingtips.

The T10M-9 development aircraft in late camouflage.

27

The Su-27SMK demonstrator at KnAAPO's factory airfield in Komsomol'sk-on-Amur.

The Su-27SK entered production in Komsomol'sk-on-Amur in 1991. Deliveries to China's People's Liberation Army Air Force (PLAAF) began in 1992.

The more capable Su-35 and Su-37 were also more expensive, and few nations could afford them – a point not to be treated lightly, considering that most nations ordering Soviet/Russian military hardware were not rich. Hence a more capable version of the Su-27SK designated Su-27SMK was developed as a cheaper alternative to the Su-35/Su-37, the M standing for *modernizeerovannyy* (upgraded). In similar fashion to the Su-35/Su-37, it possessed both counter-air and strike capability.

Changes as compared to the Su-27SK include two extra underwing hardpoints increasing the ordnance load from 6,000 kg (13,227 lb) to 8,000 kg (17,636 lb) and an improved targeting, navigation, communications and ECM suite. Two of the pylons are 'wet', permitting the carriage of 2,000-litre (440 Imperial gallon) drop tanks, and a retractable IFR probe is provided.

The Su-27SMK features an improved version of the N-001 pulse-Doppler fire control radar with better air-to-air and air-to-ground capability. Besides the usual R-27 and R-73 AAMs, weapons options include up to eight R-77 (RVV-AE) medium-range AAMs, up to six Kh-29TD TV-guided AGMs, Kh-29L or S-25LD laser-guided AGMs (the latter type is developed by KB Tochmash, ie, *Konstrooktorskoye byuro tochnovo mashi-nostroyeniya* – Precision Machinery Design Bureau), up to four Kh-31P anti-radiation missiles (alternatively, Zvezda Kh-25PD ARMs on twin ejector racks), and one or two Kh-59M tactical cruise missiles The fighter can also carry up to six KAB-500KR TV-guided 'smart bombs'. Western avionics and/or weapons may be integrated at customer request.

The Su-27SKs already delivered are to be upgraded to Su-27SMK standard in two stages. First, the extra hardpoints, 'wet' pylons and IFR capability will be introduced and R-77 (RVV-AE) AAMs integrated. The second stage involves integration of improved avionics and guided air-to-ground weapons.

KnAAPO used a Su-27 painted in a PLAAF-style slate-grey colour scheme (but with a white radome not found on Chinese Flankers) as a Su-27SMK demonstrator. However, apart from two extra pylons and Cyrillic '27SMK' writ large in dark blue on the nose, this aircraft is little different from standard Su-27s, lacking the refuelling probe and the other advanced features which the factory did not install because higher-priority orders had to be filled. Currently it appears that the Su-27SMK upgrade programme will go ahead only if confirmed orders are secured.

Surprisingly enough, Indonesia also considered purchasing the Su-27/Su-30. No Russian-built aircraft had been operated by the Indonesian Air Force (*Tentara Nasional Indonesia – Angkatan Udara*, or TNI-AU since President Dr Soekarno was unseated by the staunchly anti-Communist Gen Soeharto in 1966 and relations with the Soviet Union went sour. Another upgrade of the *H-B* was jointly developed by Sukhoi and KnAAPO for the TNI-AU. In the Russian press this aircraft has been referred to as the Su-30KI (despite being a single-seater), the Su-27KI (the I obviously standing for Indonesia) and simply as a 'modified Su-27SK'.

The uncoded Su-30KI prototype (c/n 36911040102, f/n 40-02) was completed in 1998, making its first flight on 28th June at the hands of KnAAPO test pilot Yevgeniy Revoonov. Outwardly the fighter differs from the standard Su-27 Flanker-B only in having a retractable refuelling probe on the port side of the nose. Other changes to the equipment include an upgraded N-001M radar capable of working with R-77 (RVV-AE) missiles, the addition of a global positioning system (GPS), a Western-standard automatic approach and instrument landing system (ILS/VOR). Kh-29T AGMs, Kh-31P ARMs, Kh-59M cruise missiles, KAB-500Kr/KAB-500L and KAB-1500Kr/KAB-1500L guided bombs were to be integrated later on for the air-to-ground role; the maximum ordnance load is 8,000 kg (17,636 lb).

Russian sources say that the Su-30KI is almost identical to the Boeing (McDonnell Douglas) F-15C Eagle as far as the main design criteria are concerned; eg, the Eagle's thrust/weight ratio is slightly smaller but specific wing loading is slightly lower. It should be noted that some F-15s were reengined with Pratt & Whitney F100-PW-229 or General Electric F110-GE-129 turbofans providing an aggregate thrust increase of nearly 5,000 kgp (11,000 lb st) in full afterburner, which enhanced their acceleration and turning characteristics. Nevertheless, the Su-30KI's statically unstable, blended wing/body layout, FBW controls adaptive leading-edge flaps and some other features give it better combat manoeuvrability in the long run. Another US competitor, the Lockheed Martin F-16C Block 30, has better subsonic acceleration and good turning caharcteristics but is unlikely to gain an advantage over the Flanker in an unstable turn due to its higher wing loading.

Range on internal fuel is another important aspect of modern fighter design, since carrying drop tanks restricts the weapons load. In this respect the Su-30KI wins by a length, so to say: its unrefuelled range is 1.8 to 2.3 times better than that of its Western fourth-generation counterparts. For instance, effective range in air superiority configuration is reportedly 40% longer than the F-15C's and 130% (!) longer than that of the Boeing (McDD) F/A-18C Hornet, Dassault Mirage 2000-5 and SAAB JAS-39 Gripen.

Piloted by Sukhoi OKB test pilot Viktor G. Pugachov, the Su-30KI (Su-27KI) took part in the flying display at the MAKS-99 airshow on 19th August 1999. The fighter sported an unusual black/slate grey/pale grey 'splatter camouflage', along with 'Sukhoi – KnAAPO' and 'Su-27 Family' titles. Interestingly, the colouring of the radome was identical to that of Chinese Su-27SKs (with a characteristically kinked colour division line), apart from some vertical stripes which are presumably photo calibration markings. In December the aircraft took part in the LIMA'99 airshow held at Langkawi AB, Kuala Lumpur. A few months later it was on show at the DSA'2000 defence fair held in Kuala Lumpur on 11th-14th April 2000; this show was off limits to the general public.

Negotiations with Indonesia on the purchase of Flankers dragged on for years – and came to nothing, mainly because the TNI-AU was having severe financial problems. On consideration, this was probably just as well – the deal would have been politically damaging for Russia, since Indonesia was then subjected to international ostracism because of the hostilities in East Timor.

From Trainer to Jack of all Trades

Two-seat Multi-Role Fighters

Operational experience with single-seat interceptors (including the Flanker-B) showed that in a modern dogfight the workload was simply too high for a single pilot, who had to fly the jet and operate the weapons control system while experiencing high G loads. The problem was perhaps especially acute on the Su-27, considering its impressive fuel load and long range; the pilot would feel like a squeezed lemon when the day was done.

Besides, the capabilities of today's avionics are more than one pilot can handle in a dogfight (to paraphrase a well-known election principle, one man, one brain). A second crew member was clearly needed to reduce pilot workload. In addition, providing dual flight controls enabled the crew to operate more efficiently during long sorties. One pilot would fly the aircraft, control the weapons and take care of the close-in fighting while the other would be the weapons systems operator (WSO), detecting and destroying the enemy at long range. He could also take over if the guy in the driver's seat was wounded or tired out. This led to the development of a whole range of new two-seat tactical aircraft based on the Su-27UB combat trainer.

Cuts in the Soviet Air Force's fighter fleet, the emergence of new and more stringent requirements to interceptors, the sheer length of the Soviet Union's northern borders and the scarcity of airbases in the northern regions of the country, as well as of airborne command posts (ABCPs) and airborne early warning and control (AEW&C) aircraft, placed high demands on the IA PVO. This, and the considerations described above, prompted the Sukhoi OKB to develop Su-27UB trainer into a specialised two-seat interceptor.

As well as acting on its own, the aircraft could operate as a tactical airborne command post *en miniature*, the WSO giving directions to other aircraft during concerted action. To this end a tactical situation display in the rear cockpit and other appropriate avionics (eg, data link) would be installed. Flight refuelling capability became a must in this situation.

Top and above: The T10PU-5 development aircraft, the prototype of the Su-30 interceptor.

Unlike the Su-27UB, the T10PU-5 prototype featured flight refuelling capability, improved FBW flight controls and an upgraded weapons control system.

Above, left and right: Su-30s in the final assembly shop of the Irkutsk Aircraft Production Association (IAPO).

Work on a two-seat interceptor/ABCP version of the Su-27 began in the mid-1980s, with I. V. Yemel'yanov as chief project engineer. The Su-27UB with its large internal fuel volume and heavy armament comprising ten AAMs was chosen as the starting point. The encouraging results obtained with the abovementioned modified second prototype Su-27UB (02 Blue), including the non-stop cross-country flights of 1987-88, showed that the Su-27P had room for improvement.

Working together with local engineers, a group of Sukhoi OKB engineers headed by V. Makritskiy specialists converted two standard Su-27UBs at IAPO in the summer and autumn of 1988. Coded 05 Blue and 06 Blue, the proof-of-concept aircraft were designated T10PU-5 and T10PU-6 respectively and bore the IAPO in-house designation 'izdeliye

10-4PU'; both had the standard Flanker two-tone blue camouflage. (*Izdeliye* (product) such and such is a term often used for coding Soviet military hardware items. The PU suffix is sometimes deciphered as [*voz-doosh*nyy] *poonkt oopravleniya* – airborne command post, but this is a statement open to doubt; *perekhvaht*chik *oosovershenstvo-vannyy* (interceptor, improved) appears more likely.) New features included a retractable refuelling probe (which required the IRST/LR 'ball' to be offset to starboard), a new navigation suite and changes to the FBW controls, life support and weapons control systems.

Special tooling had to be designed and manufactured for some manufacturing operations. This, and cramming the new equipment into the old 'shell' of the standard Su-27UB, was the hardest part of the job. The conver-

sion job took six months to accomplish; the T10PU-5 entered flight test in the autumn of 1988. Initially the aircraft were flown by IAPO test pilots (G. Ye. Boolanov, V. B. Maksimenkov, S. V. Makarov and N. N. Ivanov). Later, 05 Blue and 06 Blue were flown to LII for further trials.

Since no changes were made to the aerodynamics, the new interceptor was almost identical in performance and handling to the stock Su-27UB combat trainer. The aircraft passed its trials programme with flying colours and was cleared for production at IAPO as the Su-30.

Launching full-scale production posed quite a few problems. IAPO's chief engineer A. I. Fyodorov (who went on to become General Director), his deputy (structural engineering) Yuriy P. Faberovskiy, chief of

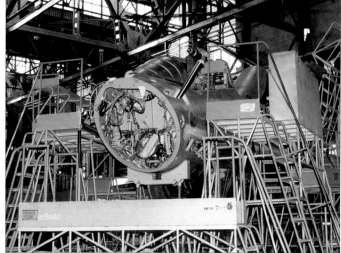

Above and right: More Su-30s nearing completion at IAPO. Note the temporary nose gear strut and protective cover on the radar antenna (bottom photo).

Manufacturing Technologies A. A. Obraztsov and Production Design Section (SKO – *Sereeynyy konstrooktorskiy otdel*) chief V. A. Goodkov had to deal with them as they came.

Finally, on 14th April 1992 the first production Su-30 (c/n 79371010101, f/n 01-01) took off from the factory's runway with Boolanov and Maksimenkov at the controls. Air Force test pilot (1st Class) Col V. Podgornyy (later promoted to Distinguished test pilot) and pilots L. G. Smelyy and A. V. Matooshin also contributed a lot to the Su-30's test programme.

The tremendous effort of IAPO's engineers, especially those responsible for assembly and testing procedures and the SKO staff, culminated in a unique combat aircraft. Unlike the single-seat Su-27, the Su-30 was not merely an air superiority fighter. Its missions included long-range combat air patrol (CAP) and escort duties, AEW&C, and pilot training. While being capable of performing the same tasks as the Su-27UB, the new aircraft had a much greater combat radius and endurance and could operate more effectively in a group of fighters by virtue of its airborne command post function. These enhanced capabilities are provided by the flight refuelling, long-range radio navigation (LORAN) and data link systems, as well as the modified life support equipment.

The Su-30 retains the excellent agility of the other members of the Flanker family; like the other versions of the Su-27, it can perform the so-called dynamic deceleration manoeuvre (better known as the Pugachov Cobra). New air-to-air weapons have greatly increased its combat potential. On internal fuel only (9,400 kg/20,723 lb) it has a range of 3,600 km (2,000 nm); with aerial refuelling, range and endurance is limited only by how much the crew can take, though a ten-hour mission time limit has been set by advice of

medical specialists. Measures have been taken to enhance crew comfort.

Still, there is always a 'but'. The collapse of the Soviet Union and ensuing economic difficulties have caused Su-30 production to go at a trickle. The very few production aircraft built to date are in service with the PVO. A notable exception is the first two production Su-30s (c/ns 79371010101 and 79371010102, f/ns 01-01 and 01-02 respectively) which were delivered to Anatoliy N. Kvochur's *Ispytahteli* (Test Pilots) display team at LII after completing their trials programme; the purchase was financed by the Jupiter Insurance Group. They are sometimes referred to as 'Su-27PUs' by the popular press – a designation which never existed.

Painted in a striking blue/red/white colour scheme and coded 596 White and 597 White, the Su-30s of the *Ispytahteli* display team made their first public performance at MosAeroShow-92, Russia's first 'real' major airshow staged at Zhukovskiy on 11th-16th August. In addition to group and solo aerobatics, the two Su-30s and the Su-27IB fighter-bomber prototype, 42 Blue (more of which later) made a refuelling demonstration, formating with the prototype IL-78M tanker, CCCP-76701 (c/n 0063471139, f/n 5405). Speaking of which, this was the first time when an IL-78 refuelled three tactical aircraft at once (usually it is either one heavy bomber or one/two tactical aircraft). Interestingly, unlike earlier demos of the same kind, all three fighters actually 'hit the tanker' in a simulated refuelling instead of flying a short way behind.

Since then the *Ispytahteli* have become regular participants at various airshows. The two Su-30s were augmented by a Su-27P (595 White, c/n 36911037511, f/n 37-11?) and the aforementioned Su-27PD (598 White, c/n 36911037820, f/n 37-20). They opened the demonstration flight sessions at

MAKS-97. One of the demos involved a formation flypast by Su-30 '597 White' and Su-24M '11 White' (c/n 1141613?); the latter was equipped with an UPAZ-1A 'buddy' refuelling pack, making a simulated refuelling of the Flanker.

Most of the production Su-30s are operated by the IA PVO's 148th Operational Conversion Unit (TsBP i PLS – *Tsentr boyevoy podgotovki i pereoochivaniya lyotnovo sostahva*, Combat and Conversion Training Centre) at Savostleyka AB near Nizhniy Novgorod. These include aircraft coded 50 Blue (c/n 96310107035), 51 Blue (c/n 96310107037), 52 Blue (c/n 96310107023), 53 Blue (c/n 96310104007) and 54 Blue (c/n 96310104010) manufactured during 1994-96. Most of them sport a fin badge depicting a shield with St. George and the dragon superimposed on the Russian flag.

(**Note:** The construction numbers of most Irkutsk-built Flankers are deciphered as follows. 963 is the factory code; 101 is the product code of the Su-30. (By comparison, the c/ns of IAPO-built Su-27UBs begin with 963104, ie, 'pure' *izdeliye* 10-4 as opposed to *izdeliye* 10-4PU?) The remaining five digits do not signify **anything at all**; the idea is to confuse would-be spies so that the c/n would not reveal the batch number and the number of the aircraft in the batch (and hence how many have been built). The first two and the last three of these 'famous last five', as they are often called, accrue independently.)

The Su-30 had its international debut when two aircraft from Savostleyka, '52 Blue' and '54 Blue', participated in the Royal International Air Tattoo '97. Escorted by a Russian Air Force IL-76MD *Candid-B* support aircraft, the fighters arrived at RAF Fairford, the traditional RIAT showground, via Chkalovsk AB near Kaliningrad on 16th July 1997. Predictably, the Su-30s drew crowds both in the static park and during the flying display when one of the fighters flown by pilot Col Yevgeniy Tikhomeerov and WSO Lt Col Mikhail Romanov gave a spirited performance.

On the way home the Russian trio had a near-miss with an airliner climbing out from London. Of course this was an unfortunate event, but near-misses are nothing out of the ordinary. Imagine the ballyhoo raised the following day by the Moscow daily *Moskovskiy Komsomolets* which ran a front-page news item titled 'Our fighters nearly shot down an airliner!'. The 'yellow press' is the same all over, and *Moskovskiy Komsomolets* has quite a reputation for its... er... *light tan colour*.

In July 1998 a group of twelve 148th TsBP i PLS pilots commanded by the Centre's deputy CO Col Martin Karapetyan flew two Mikoyan MiG-31B *Foxhound* interceptors and four Su-30s during an experiment staged to explore the combat potential of the two types during ultra-long missions (up to 10 hours). The flight involved simulated interceptions against target aircraft in the northern regions of Russia and live missile launches against target drones at the Ashuluk PVO target range in southern Russia. Apart from the interceptors, the experiment involved two IL-78 tankers and an Il'yushin/Beriyev A-50 *Mainstay* AWACS aircraft which loitered in a predesignated location, monitoring air traffic over a large area and co-ordinating the fighters' actions.

The pair of MiG-31Bs which took off from the airbase in Pravdinsk (a short way north of Nizhniy Novgorod) acted as the first line of defence. Using their unique Phazotron N-007 (SBI-16) *Zaslon* (Shield) radars, the *Foxhounds* detected incoming 'enemy aircraft' up to 200 km (124 miles) away, passing target information by data link to the Su-30s following 60 km (37 miles) behind. The fast and agile Su-30s would then ignite the afterburners and make a high-speed dash to attack as required.

The 8,500-km (5,280-mile) route lay across the European part of Russia. During the ten-hour flight the interceptors were thrice refuelled by IL-78 tankers. Additional data for

A production Su-30 belonging to the Russian Air Defence Force's 148th TsBP i PLS (Savostleyka AB) prepares to tak on fuel from an IL-78 tanker.

the fighter crews was provided by the A-50. The *Foxhounds* and Flankers operated in varying formations, depending on the mission details.

148th TsBP i PLS MiG-31Bs and Su-30s participated in a joint command and staff exercise staged by the IA PVO and the Russian Air Force's strategic bomber arm (DA, *dahl'nyaya aviahtsiya* – long-range aviation) in the summer of 1999, escorting Tupolev Tu-95MS *Bear-H* and Tu-160 *Blackjack* missile carriers to the target range on Novaya Zemlya (New Land) Island, a former nuclear test range. A short while earlier, in early April 1999, an experimental exercise took place during which MiG-31B and Su-30 crews each spent eight hours in the air, making a total of 12 contacts with IL-78 tankers.

An export version of the Su-30 appeared before long. By analogy with the Su-27SK it was designated Su-30K (*kommehrcheskiy*) or *izdeliye* 10-4PK. The Su-30K differs only slightly from Russian Air Force examples in identification friend-or-foe (IFF), navigation and communications equipment.

On 20th April 1994 a Russian-Indian working group convened in New Delhi to discuss co-operation in aerospace matters. One of the items on the agenda was possible licence production of the Su-30MK (see next entry) by Hindustan Aeronautics Ltd. (HAL) which already had a history of building Soviet fighters. On 30th November 1996, after more than two years of negotiations, a contract was signed in Irkutsk for the delivery of 40 Su-30K/MKs to the Indian Air Force. The aircraft were to be delivered in four batches over a five-year period during which the Su-30 would be progressively upgraded.

IAF pilots and ground crews took conversion training at Sukhoi's flight test facility in Zhukovskiy in January-April 1997, with Viktor G. Pugachov acting as instructor pilot. The first four Su-30Ks for the IAF were completed ahead of schedule in mid-March 1997. On 19th March, 26th March, 9th April and 15th April four Russian Air Force Antonov An-124 Ruslan (*Condor*) freighters arrived at Lohegaon AB near Pune (Poona), Maharashtra, carrying two dismantled fighters each. The eight Su-30Ks were reassembled and test flown by IAPO personnel.

Meanwhile, Chief of India's Air Staff, Air Marshal Satish Kumar Sarina visited Russia in late March 1997. Among other things, he called at IAPO to inspect the construction of Su-30Ks for the IAF. On 31st March Air Marshal Sarina met Russian Air Force C-in-C Col Gen Pyotr S. Deynekin in Moscow to discuss co-operation between Russia and India in defence matters.

On 11th June the IAF held an official ceremony at Lohegaon AB to mark the service entry of the Su-30K and the first eight aircraft (serialled SB 001 through SB 008) were declared fully operational with the 24 Sqn –

Top and above: The crew of a 148th TsBP i PLS Su-30 practises flight refuelling techniques.

the first IAF unit to operate the type. Guests of honour included Prime Minister Shri Gujal, Air Marshal Sarina (who had by then become Indian Air Force C-in-C), Russian ambassador Albert Chernyshov, Rosvo'orouzheniye State Company Deputy General Director Oleg Sidorenko and former IAPO General Director Aleksey Fyodorov. Speaking at the ceremony, Air Marshal Sarina described 11th June 1997 as 'a notable day in IAF history', stating that 'the Su-30K is an advanced fighter built to meet the Air Force's current and future demands in full'.

(**Note:** *Rosvo'orouzheniye* was Russia's principal arms export agency at the time (the name translates as Russian Weapons). In late 2000 it merged with Promexport (= Industrial Export), another arms exporter, to create **Rosoboronex**port (Russian Defence Exports), as the government decided that having two competing companies officially representing Russia on the world arms market was pointless and even damaging.)

On January 26, 1998 the traditional military parade was held in the streets of New Delhi as part of the Republic Day celebrations. For the first time IAF Su-30Ks (painted in Indian flag colours for the occasion) partic-

ipated in the event, drawing considerable attention with a lively aerobatics display.

On March 22, 1998 the aircraft were used operationally for the first time. Three Su-30Ks participated in the *Vayu Shakti-98* exercise in Pokhran, Rajasthan. The fighters demolished 11 targets, including a mock runway, with pinpoint bomb strikes. The Su-30 amazed the audience, which included some 25 foreign military attachés, with an aerobatics display which culminated in a mock dogfight with a MiG-29 *Fulcrum-A*. The show was not without political innuendoes. A senior IAF official was quoted as saying that 'there has been uninformed criticism of the Su-30's combat capabilities and we wanted to put that to rest once and for all'.

Indonesia also considered purchasing the Su-30K when a deal involving the delivery of F-16s to the Indonesian Air Force fell through. Indonesian Air Force C-in-C Air Marshal Sutria Tubagus described the Su-30 as being the most effective and economical to operate and having the biggest combat radius of the four fighters on the TNI-AU shortlist.

Initially the order was to be for 12 aircraft with an option for eight more; in the course of

603 Black outline, the Su-30MK demonstrator (the first aircraft to have this designation) at LII's airfield in Zhukovskiy.

the negotiations Indonesia expressed an interest in a single-seat version of the Su-30 – the so-called Su-30KI described in the previous chapter. Eventually, however, the deal failed to materialise.

The Su-30 was primarily designed for the IA PVO which could use its capabilities as a long-range patrol fighter and interceptor to the full. However, new precision air-to-surface missiles (including anti-shipping missiles) became available to the VVS and the naval air arm (AVMF – *Aviahtsiya voyenno-morskovo flota*) in the early 1990s. All of Russia's leading military aircraft manufacturers, including Sukhoi, started work on delivery platforms for these weapons.

Considering the importance of aviation in modern warfare, Sukhoi proposed a tactical strike aircraft based on the Su-30. The wide range of weapons, air-to-ground capability and new avionics options gave the Su-30MK, as the aircraft was designated (the implications are obvious), considerable export potential.

The proposal was put forth in 1993; same year the Su-30MK prototype made its international debut at the 40th Paris Air Show. The aircraft was converted from the first production Su-30 previously operated by the

Ispytahteli display team (ex-597 White, c/n 79371010101). Upon conversion it received a disruptive sand/brown desert camouflage and a new low-visibility tactical code, 603 Black outline.

The Su-30MK has a 8,000-kg (17,636-lb) ordnance load; ten pylons out of twelve can carry guided missiles. Vympel R-27R1/R-27ER, R-27T1/R-27ET, R-77 (RVV-AE) medium-range AAMs and R-73/R-73E short-range AAMs with all-aspect IR or radar seeker heads are carried for air-to-air engagements. The aircraft can attack ground targets and surface ships with Zvezda Kh-31P anti-radiation missiles, Zvezda Kh-25ML (AS-10 *Karen*) and Vympel Kh-29T/Kh-29L TV- and laser-guided ASMs, Raduga Kh-59M TV-guided cruise missiles and KAB-500 guided bombs, as well as free-fall bombs and unguided rockets.

The precision weapons enhance the Su-30MK's capabilities a good deal. For instance, the Kh-59M can transmit a 'bomb's eye view' (the picture seen by its TV guidance system) to the WSO's display at a distance in excess of 100 km (55 nm). Having located the target, the WSO can guide the missile manually all the way in and score a direct hit. The Kh-59M was developed under General

Designer Igor' Seleznyov, aided by Viktor Galooshko who was in charge of the weapons control system design effort. Conversely, the Kh-29T is a 'fire-and-forget' (or, as some authors put it, 'wish 'em dead') missile. The WSO just sets the crosshairs on the target and pushes the Memory Lock button; everything else is automatic.

The Kh-29L and S-29L are guided by means of a man-portable laser designator; it is up to the man on the ground to point the beam at the correct target. The Kh-31P ARM can take out all types of air defence (AD) radars while the aircraft stays well out of range of the surface-to-air missiles controlled by the radars; thus, the Su-30MK can fill the SEAD (suppression of enemy air defences, or 'Wild Weasel') role as well. Finally, like all versions of the Flanker, the aircraft has a 30-mm (1.18 calibre) Gryazev/Shipoonov GSh-301 rapid-firing single-barrel cannon (aka TKB-678 or 9A4071) with 150 rounds installed in the starboard LERX. This is a potent weapon with a 1,500-rpm rate of fire. (TKB = *Tool'skoye konstrooktorskoye byuro* – Toola [Weapons] Design Bureau, aka NPO *Tochnost'* (Accuracy), in Toola south of Moscow, a city renowned for its makers of firearms.)

The weapons control system was to feature a new-generation coherent pulse-Doppler radar with a 1-m (3 ft 3.37 in.) scanner. It was to track ten aerial targets at up to 100 km (55 nm), guiding missiles to two priority threats at up to 65 km (36 nm). The WCS was to automatically download target data to the missiles and fire them at preset intervals and in a preset sequence. The pilots were to use helmet-mounted sights; target data would also be presented on the direct vision display and HUD. The aircraft is also equipped with an IRST unit with day/night channels and a laser ranger. Western avionics and/or weapons would be integrated at customer request.

The precision weapons required not only changes to the WCS but additional guidance equipment allowing them to be used day and night in any kind of weather. Fitting this equipment proved to be tricky – there was just no room to spare. As a result, part of the equipment (eg, the laser rangefinder/designator and infra-red intelligence gear for night/poor weather operations) had to be carried in interchangeable pods in the manner of the USAF's Pave Something-or-other systems (Pave Knife, Pave Tack etc.).

Both cockpits of the Su-30MK feature identical sets of flight and weapons controls, enabling either of the two crewmen to fly the aircraft or use the weapons at any time. Task distribution between the pilot and WSO ('front seat flies, back seat fires') reduces crew workload and increases the chances of mission success, even if the crew is not very skilled. On-station time during CAP missions is 10 hours.

The Su-30MK was displayed again at the IDEX'93 airshow in Dubai. Since then the aircraft has been a regular participant at international airshows and has kept amazing the aviation world with its capabilities. Among other things, 603 Black outline was one of the highlights of the FIDAE'94 airshow in Santiago de Chile, flying across the Atlantic ocean *on internal fuel only* – a sensation in itself. That year it was demonstrated at two other international airshows – ILA'94 (at Berlin-Schönefeld) and Farnborough International '94. On the latter occasion the Su-30MK put on such an impressive aerobatics display with a full load of bombs and rockets that competitors had to admit no Western aircraft could match it. The aircraft was also present at the MAKS-93 and MAKS-95 airshows in Zhukovskiy, as well as airshows in China, Malaysia and India.

Still, the Su-30MK remains in prototype form as of this writing, even though IAPO has had a complete set of manufacturing drawings and documents for several years. The reason keeping it from entering production was lack of orders: the Russian Ministry of Defence had no money and, strangely enough, no interest in the fighter.

The Su-30MK demonstrator wore three-tone desert camouflage.

Front view of the Su-30MK demonstrator.

The Su-30 demonstrator in front of Sukhoi's hangar in Zhukovskiy.

The Su-30 'cleans up' on take-off (top)...

...and streams its twin brake 'chutes on landing.

Initial deliveries under the Indian contract were Su-30Ks differing from Russian AF Su-30s only slightly in avionics fit. Starting in the year 2000, however, IAPO and Sukhoi were to upgrade the Su-30K to improve its agility, performance and firepower considerably. The result was effectively a next-generation aircraft. New features included automatically-controlled canards *a la* Su-27M (Su-35) for better low-speed/high-alpha handling, AL-31FP engines with axisymmetrical thrust-vectoring nozzles for ultra-manoeuvrability, and a completely new mission avionics suite giving the fighter counter-air, air-to-ground and maritime strike capability.

The fighter received the designation Su-30MKI (*indeeyskiy* – Indian) or *izdeliye* 10-4PMK-2 to distinguish it from the original Su-30MK lacking canards and TVC. The Su-30Ks delivered initially would be updated to Su-30MKI standard in due time.

The Sukhoi OKB was open for international co-operation when it came to choosing the avionics. Under the contract India would not just take delivery of the fighters but have

Sukhoi test pilot Igor' V. Votintsev poses beside the Su-30MK (the first aircraft to bear this designation).

a hand in developing the Su-30MKI's avionics suite to fit the requirements of the IAF. Of course, Sukhoi would still have overall programme responsibility for the 'international' avionics suite, ensuring that the components 'got along' and the suite met contract specifications, no matter where the avionics were

sourced. And of course, the company used well-established co-operation schemes with Russian component suppliers who are traditional Sukhoi partners, as well as with Russian Air Force technical experts, when developing the Su-30MKI.

The avionics suite included a new multi-mode fire control radar capable of tracking 15 aerial targets while guiding missiles to four priority threats and having high resistance to ground clutter. This was linked to a new multi-mode optoelectronic navigation/attack system featuring an inertial navigation system (INS) with laser gyros and a satellite navigation system (GPS). The Su-30MKI also featured a new cockpit indication system with high-resolution liquid-crystal colour MFDs, plus an entirely new flight data recorder (FDR) which, apart from its primary function, recorded tactical information as well.

The armament comprised AAMs with all-aspect SARH and IR seeker heads, anti-radiation missiles, TV-guided AGMs and 'smart bombs' and a wide array of unguided air-to-surface weapons.

The contract required the Su-30MKI upgrade programme to proceed in parallel with Su-30K deliveries. Actually, however, Sukhoi started work a full year before the papers were signed. The money India paid up front for the Su-30Ks was used to fund research by Sukhoi and NPO Lyul'ka-Saturn and to initiate production at IAPO (manufacture jigs and tooling, procure materials and so on).

In the spring of 1997 a production Su-30 coded 56 Blue was converted into the first prototype Su-30MKI at Sukhoi's experimental shop. The aircraft received the in-house designation T10PMK-1; hence the tactical code was later changed to 01 Blue. Outward recognition features were the canards (initially painted in black and yellow 'take care' stripes on the first prototype), a twin-wheel nose gear unit *a la* Su-35 and the vectoring nozzles which 'bled' down to maximum downward deflection after engine shutdown. Somewhat misleadingly, the prototype carried a small 'Su-30MK' (not MKI) logo on the fins.

On 23rd April the aircraft arrived at Sukhoi's flight test facility at LII, Zhukovskiy. Ground systems tests began in May and took nearly two months. Finally, on 1st July 1997 the Su-30MKI made a 50-minute first flight at the hands of Sukhoi test pilot (1st Class) Vyacheslav Yu. Aver'yanov who had also flown the Su-35 and Su-37. Stability and handling trials continued into early 1998.

Originally the T10PMK-1 was powered by 12,800-kgp (28,218 lb st) AL-31FU engines with pitch/yaw thrust vectoring, but these went unserviceable or ran out of service life during early flight tests. Since identical engines were unavailable, less powerful AL-31FPs with pitch-only thrust vectoring (±15°)

Top and above: The ill-starred first prototype Su-30MKI, 01 Blue, on LII's runway.

had to be fitted as a stopgap measure. Unlike the Su-37, however, the TVC nozzle hinges were tilted 32° outward from the horizontal plane. Thus the nozzles generated a side force when deflected differentially, improving the fighter's agility and control response at near-zero speeds. The nozzle petal actuators were powered by the fuel system, not hydraulically. The AL-31FPs installed on 56 Blue were prototype engines which had seen a lot of bench testing.

In 1998 a pre-production Su-27UB trainer coded 06 Blue – the sixth Flanker-C built (T10PU-6) – was converted into the second prototype Su-30MK at Sukhoi's experimental shop, joining the trials programme on 23rd March. For some obscure reason this aircraft was redesignated T10PMK-6 (rather than T10PMK-2) and the original tactical code was retained. (The prototypes were sometimes referred to as the Su-30MK-1 and Su-30MK-6 respectively.) Unlike the first prototype, 06 Blue had a standard single-wheel nose gear unit.

The Su-30MKI was shown publicly for the first time on 16th August 1998 when 01 Blue participated in the annual Aviation Day fly-past at Moscow's Tushino airfield with V. Aver'yanov at the controls. (Aviation Day is celebrated on the third Sunday of August.) Unfortunately, the display was brief and low clouds hid the aircraft from sight every now and then. The 'dress rehearsal' on 15th

August had been much longer. In November 1998 the type had its international debut when the same aircraft was displayed at the Aero India '98 airshow in Bangalore.

In June 1999 the first prototype arrived in Le Bourget where it was to participate in the 43rd Paris Air Show (13th-20th June). By

At first the prototype retained its original tactical code 56 Blue. Note unpainted new nose gear door.

37

Top, centre and above: Indian Air Force representatives inspect the Su-30MKI in Zhukovskiy.

Above: Close-up of the Su-30MKI's vectoring nozzles

Right above, centre and below: Three more views of the Su-30MKI prototype.

then the T10PMK-1 and the T10PMK-6 had made more than 140 flights between them, mainly under aerodynamics and TVC test programmes; exploration of the flight envelope in ultra-manoeuvrability mode proceeded in parallel. Pilot Vyacheslav Aver'yanov and WSO Vladimir G. Shendrik made three demo flights and the Su-30MKI qualified for the flying display. Both aviation experts and 'plain Joe' visitors were anxious to see the latest Sukhoi fighter fly at the show.

Unfortunately, on 12th June 1999 the Su-30MKI crashed during a training flight prior to the grand opening. While demonstrating a controlled spin which was part of the

display programme, Aver'yanov initiated recovery too late, making one turn too many. As it pulled out of the dive, the fighter struck the ground in a tail-down attitude; next moment it was climbing away, but with the starboard engine jetpipe broken by the impact and flames belching from the port engine due to a ruptured fuel line. The damaged starboard engine nozzle was pointing about 30° up (twice its design limit), causing an uncontrollable pitch-up. As the Su-30MKI stood on its tail and the nose started falling through, Aver'yanov and Shendrik ejected. Seconds later the fighter pancaked out beside the runway and exploded – an eerie

05 Blue, the first pre-production Su-30MK, inside Sukhoi's hangar at LII, Zhukovskiy.

This dramatic sequence shot by Helmut Walther depicts the last moments of Su-30MKI '01 Blue' as it crashes at Le Bourget on 12th June 1999.

replay of Anatoliy Kvochur's accident in a MiG-29 *Fulcrum-A* at the 1989 Paris Air Show.

The crew was rushed to a hospital but released the following day, as neither Aver'yanov nor Shendrik had suffered any injuries. The accident report was never published, but even then aviation experts agreed that the crash was caused by pilot error (Aver'yanov later said that 'disorientation caused by the sun affecting the pilot's perception of height above the ground' had been the cause).

Nevertheless, the loss of the T10PMK-1 did not damage the reputation of the Su-30MKI or the relationship with the Indian Air

The same aircraft following modifications and repaint, seen on LII's runway.

This page and opposite: The first prototype Su-30MKI takes off from Zhukovskiy.

Opposite page, above and centre: The second prototype Su-30MKI (06 Blue) takes off.

Opposite page, below: The first prototype Su-30 with bombs during a test flight.

This page: The second Su-30MKI on the ground and in flight.

The second prototype Su-30MKI shortly after a demonstration flight at Zhukovskiy.

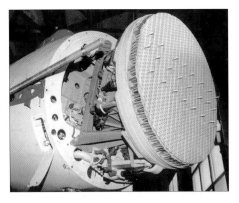

Force which had ordered the aircraft. Moreover, Vyacheslav Aver'yanov flew the second prototype daily during MAKS-99, giving the most spectacular flying display of the show (in everyone's opinion) on his home ground. One has to give credit both to Sukhoi's top executives who, despite the Paris mishap, trusted him to fly the second and then only surviving Su-30MKI, and to Aver'yanov who 'found his nerve' very quickly after the accident – clearing both the aircraft and himself completely.

Under the abovementioned contract the Su-30Ks already in service with the Indian Air Force will be upgraded to Su-30MKI standard in two stages. Stage A involves installation of canards and new avionics (and apparently the twin-wheel nose gear unit to cater for the increased weight of the latter). AL-31FP thrust-vectoring engines will be retrofitted during Stage B; these have now reached an adequate reliability level and can be installed in any production Flanker without any problems. The production-standard Su-30MKI is to feature a Russian WCS built around the NIIP N-011M Bars multi-mode phased-array radar. Also, the Urals Optomechanical Plant (UOMZ – *Oorahl'skiy optiko-mekhanicheskiy zavod*) in Yekaterinburg developed the OLS-30 IRST/LR unit (*optiko-lokatseeonnaya stahntsiya*) specially for the Su-30MKI. The OLS-30 has two channels (infra-red and laser) and the ability to track aerial and surface targets, determining their co-ordinates and range. It features a vibration-protected receiver, a self-contained cryogenic cooling system and new software. Field of view is 120° in azimuth and +60°/-15° in elevation; the unit weighs 182 kg (401 lb).

The third Su-30MKI coded 05 Blue was the first pre-production aircraft, featuring a complete mission avionics suite (which had been finalised by then). Wearing a three-tone grey/black camouflage, it was demonstrated with considerable success at the Aero India-2001 airshow in Bangalore on 7th-11th February 2001. Once again the fighter was flown by Vyacheslav Aver'yanov, keeping the spectators, defence observers and the Indian military enthralled by its daily demonstration flights. Chief of India's Air Staff, Air Chief Marshal Anil Y. Tipnis took a ride in the

Top left: The phased array of the NIIP N-011 Bars radar.

Top right: The Su-30MKI's engine nozzles.

Centre left: The Su-30MKI's engine nacelles. Note the bracing struts absorbing the lateral loads during thrust vectoring.

Centre right: The Su-30MKI's cockpit canopy and canards.

Left: A group of journalists inspects the still unpainted first pre-production Su-30M at IAPO.

The first prototype Su-30 (T10PU-5) following conversion as the Su-30MKK demonstrator.

Left and below: Two views of the first pre-production Su-30MK in IAPO's assembly shop.

Su-30MKI with Aver'yanov and was absolutely delighted. 'This is an outstanding aircraft!' he said as he climbed out of the cockpit. 'I've never seen anything like this in my life!' Tipnis pulled 7 Gs during some manoeuvres when he was flying the aircraft.

Deliveries of the Su-30MKI and upgrades of the Su-30Ks already delivered to the IAF to Su-30MKI standard have been delayed because of the need to finalise the fighter's avionics suite. The IAF tender eventually resulted in a mixture of Russian, French, Israeli and Indian equipment being selected. The greater part of the avionics will be supplied by the French companies SAGEM and Sextant Avionique; this goes mainly for the navigation system (including GPS) and MFD-55 and MFD-56 multi-function displays (the latter model is larger and colour, not monochrome). The choice is hardly a matter of chance, since the IAF has picked French avionics for upgrading its Mikoyan MiG-21*bis Fishbed* fighters, MiG-27M Bahadur (*Flogger-J*) and BAe Jaguar strike aircraft. The Su-30MKI's head-up displays will be supplied by the Israeli avionics house El-Op (which will probably undertake a similar upgrade of India's MiG-27Ms).

HAL has been granted a licence to build 140 Su-30MKIs. Licence production at the Nasik division is to be mastered in four stages. The first aircraft assembled from Russian-supplied components – ie, a CKD (completely-knocked-down) kit – will fly in 2004, with two more following before the end of the year. Six Su-30MKIs will be completed

Top and above: The first prototype Su-30MKI toting its maximum ordnance load in strike configuration: 32 250-kg (551-lb) FAB-250 bombs on MBD3-U6-68 multiple ejector racks and two R-73 AAMs on the wingtip pylons.

Top and above: The second Su-30MKI touches down in Zhukovskiy.

501 Blue, the first 'real' prototype Su-30MKK, seen during a test flight. Note the dielectric panels on the stabilator tips.

The same aircraft with one of the standard weapons fits: Two Kh-31P ARMs, two Kh-59M AGMs, two R-73 short-range AAMs and two R-77 (RVV-AE) medium-range AAMs.

The second and third Su-30MKKs, 502 Blue and 503 Black, formate during a test flight.

The Su-30MKK features taller, increased-area CFRP fins with integral tanks *á la* Su-35. Note the 'brandy stripes' on the fins of this one.

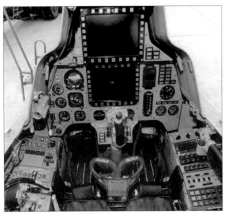

Front (top) and rear cockpits of the Su-30MKK.

Right: Still in primer, the third Su-30MKK flies echelon starboard formation with the second one.

in 2005 and another eight in 2006; after that, production will proceed at a rate of ten per year. At this stage the aircraft will be made entirely of locally manufactured items; the airframe will be built by the Nasik factory, the engines in Koraput, the radar and other electronics in Hyderabad, the flight avionics in Korv and the hydraulic and pneumatic components in Laknau. To facilitate product support Sukhoi and HAL will establish a customs warehouse which will enable any spares to be delivered to the IAF within two or three days. The US$ 3.3 billion licensing agreement provides for further upgrades, but not before actual licence production has been started.

The Su-30MKI started a new trend. Like their British and American colleagues, Russian combat aircraft designers are now creating new versions to suit the needs of a specific customer, with appropriate designation suffixes. The next spinoff of the Su-30 was developed for the PLAAF of China, hence the designation Su-30MKK (the second K stands for *kitayskiy* – Chinese). (Cf. McDonnell Douglas EAV-8B Matador (E for Espana – Spain), McDD CF-18A/B Hornet (C for Canada), or the British 'Mark something-or-other' system (eg, Westland Lynx Mk 21 for Brazil, Mk 88 for West Germany, Mk 95 for Portugal etc.) The MKK suffix earned it the nickname *makahka* (macaque) – for purely alliterative reasons (this is **not** a racist hint at the Chinese customer).

Despite having an almost identical designation, the Su-30MKK differs a lot from the Indian version both structurally and in equipment, incorporating some features of the Su-35. It lacks the canards and TVC feature of the Su-30MKI, being powered by standard AL-31Fs. On the other hand, it has the tall, thick, square-tipped CFRP fins of the Su-35 incorporating fuel tanks.

The fighter has an upgraded N-001M fire control radar which is compatible with R-77 (RVV-AE) medium-range AAMs; a new IRST/LR designed by NPO Gheofizika is also fitted. Both radar and IRST have an air-to-ground mode, allowing the Su-30MKK to deliver both unguided and high-precision guided weapons. The avionics suite is developed by Ramenskoye Instrument Design Bureau (RPKB – *Rahmenskoye pree-borostroitel'noye konstrooktorskoye byuro*). It features new-generation digital computers with the latest software linked to the main avionics subsystems and the weapons control system by multiplex databuses, as well as a 'glass cockpit' with liquid-crystal MFDs.

The Su-30MKK's combat potential is to be further enhanced by integrating Kh-59M AGMs with TV command line-of-sight guidance, Kh-29T TV-guided AGMs, Kh-31P medium-range ARMs and KAB-500Kr guided bombs. The aircraft can carry up to 8,000 kg (17,636 lb) of unguided weapons on twelve hardpoints.

The Su-30MKK prototype was converted from the very first Su-30 (T10PU-5, 05 Blue) in early 1999, making its maiden flight at LII on March 9. Surprisingly, it was decided to build the Su-30MKK at KnAAPO, which until now has produced only single-seat versions of the Flanker (apart from a few initial-production Su-27UBs), instead of IAPO which traditionally builds the two-seaters. Geographical proximity to China, the customer, may have been a factor. On the other hand, the Chinese Su-27UBKs had been built in Irkutsk and there was no real reason why the Su-30MKK should not be manufactured there as well.

The Su-35UB prototype on the runway in Zhukovskiy.

Coded 501 Blue and painted in a three-tone grey/bluish grey camouflage with appropriate 'Su-30MKK' titles on the fins, the first pre-production aircraft (sometimes described as the first 'real' prototype) took to the air in Komsomol'sk-on-Amur on 19th May 1999 at the hands of Su-30 project test pilot Vyacheslav Aver'yanov. The second pre-production aircraft (502 Blue) was completed in mid-summer; it sported a PLAAF-style slate grey colour scheme with 'Su-30MK' titles and 'five-star brandy' stripes on the fins. The third and fourth Su-30MKKs (503 Black and 504 Black) were test flown in an overall chrome yellow primer finish; the former aircraft later received the same grey colour scheme, becoming 503 Blue.

The first batch of ten production Su-30MKKs was reportedly delivered in late 2000. One of them was the the second aircraft which took part in Airshow China 2000 at Zhuhai-Sanzao airport, coded 502 White this time and wearing an overall slate grey PLAAF-style finish. Interestingly, almost simultaneously the PLAAF took delivery of four Su-27UBKs built by IAPO.

Curiously, the Su-30MKI and Su-30MKK are both referred to in-house simply as the Su-30MK. The 'customer designator' is intentionally omitted in Sukhoi press releases – ostensibly to underscore the fighter's versatility, though security reasons are probably involved as well.

On 22nd January 2001 the *Utusan Malaysia* daily reported that the Royal Malaysian Air Force (RMAF, or TUDM – *Tentera Udara Diraja Malaysia*) was in the final stages of closing a deal for the delivery of Su-30MKM fighters. No details of the Malaysian version are available as of this writing.

The Su-30MK (Su-30MKI, Su-30MKK) was not the last in the 'Su-30 series' line of fighters. KnAAPO has succeeded in developing a new two-seat multi-role version of the Flanker – the Su-35UB – on its own. The designation may suggest this is a combat trainer derivative of the Su-35 (Su-27M), but this is not exactly true. The aircraft was designed to combine the Su-37's strong points with the best features of both varieties of the Su-30MK – the MKI and the MKK. Interestingly, for the first time KnAAPO engineers made large-scale use of computer-aided design (CAD) when designing the aircraft and issuing the manufacturing drawings.

The Su-35UB is to be powered by modified AL-31FPs rated at 12,500 kgp (27,557 lb st) but featuring pitch/yaw thrust vectoring. Apart from the powerplant, it differs from the Su-30MKK in having canards and an improved radar; differences from the Su-30MKI are modified engines and square-tipped CFRP fins of increased area and thickness identical to those of the Su-30MKK and Su-35. The additional fin tanks give increased range on internal fuel.

The Su-30KN makes a demonstration flight at the MAKS-99 airshow in Zhukovskiy.

MAKS-99 was the first time a natural metal aircraft was put on display in Zhukovskiy.

The Su-30KN makes a formation take-off with the Su-27PD (598 White).

Of all Su-30 versions developed as of this writing the Su-35UB has the most sophisticated avionics suite. It is equipped with an N-011M fire control radar compatible with the entire range of AAMs, ASMs and bombs which are on – or will be added to – the Russian Air Force inventory. The aircraft has 12 weapons hardpoints and, like the other members of the 'Su-30 family', has flight refuelling capability.

The Su-35UB prototype was completed in mid-2000. Coded 801 Blue and wearing a bright blue/light blue/dark blue camouflage, this aircraft was powered by AL-31F engines at the time of its first flight, lacking TVC capability (the intended engines were apparently

Above: Close-up of the weapons carried on the pylons of the Su-30KN.

Below left: Front view of the Su-30KN; below right: The front cockpit of the same aircraft.

unavailable at the time). Flight tests began in the autumn of 2000 and the aircraft is expected to be unveiled at one of the major international airshows in 2001 (most probably MAKS-2001).

A while earlier, in 1996, the Sukhoi OKB started work on another two-seat multi-role fighter designated Su-30K2. It differs from the basic Su-30 in having a new wide forward fuselage with side-by-side seating (this arrangement was first used on the Su-27IB experimental fighter-bomber and Su-34/Su-32FN strike aircraft). Unlike these types, the Su-30K2 has a conventional ogival radome; thus it is very similar in overall appearance to the Su-27KUB naval trainer (see Chapter Four). On the other hand, the aircraft lacks the Su-27KUB's design features associated with carrier operations (wing/horizontal tail folding, arrestor hook and reinforced landing gear for no-flare landings).

Unlike the Su-34/Su-32FN (see next chapter), the Su-30K2 will be a multi-role tactical aircraft rather than a dedicated strike aircraft. To this end it will probably be equipped with the N-011M radar – one of the best Russian fire control radars as of this writing. For various reasons KnAAPO did not begin construction of several prototypes until 1999, and no tentative first flight date is known.

As already mentioned, the collapse of the Soviet Union and the resulting political turmoil triggered a lengthy economic crisis. As a result, defence spending was cut dramatically and new equipment acquisition in the Russian armed forces (including the VVS) dropped almost to zero. Ordering such expensive aircraft as the Su-35/Su-37 and Su-30MK was impossible in these conditions. Meanwhile, the Flankers already in service were growing obsolescent.

Therefore in February 1999 IAPO offered a low-cost mid-life update (MLU) programme for Russian Su-30s as a private venture – a twig on the Flanker upgrade tree, so to say. No separate designation existed at first, but from Y2K onwards the aircraft is known as the Su-30KN; nobody seems to know what the N suffix stands for. (Actually the work had been started by the Sukhoi OKB but then project chief Mikhail Korzhooyev quit Sukhoi to become IAPO Vice-President, taking the Su-30KN programme with him.)

The main effort was directed at expanding the Su-30's air-to-ground capability. In so doing the engineers chose to expand the avionics suite by adding new components rather than redesign it; this allows the aircraft's existing strengths to be retained and enhanced. To keep costs down the airframe, engines and most of the systems were left unchanged, with the addition of several new subsystems and features associated with the Su-30KN's new strike role. The navigation suite includes an extra (parallel) channel with an A-737 satellite communications receiver

compatible with both the Russian GLONASS (*globahl'naya navigatseeonnaya spootniko-vaya sistema* – global navigation satellite system) and the US NAVSTAR system. The NIIP N-001 Mech (Sword) radar has been modified to have ground mapping capability and track moving ground targets.

In both cockpits the standard cathode-ray tube (CRT) direct vision display has been replaced by a 5x5" MFI-55 (*mnogofoonkt-seeonahl'nyy indikahtor*) colour liquid-crystal MFD. This shows radar and optoelectronic targeting system imagery, tactical information or a 'bomb's eye view' generated by a TV-guided bomb or AGM. The weapons control system features a new MVK computer

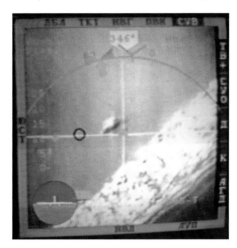

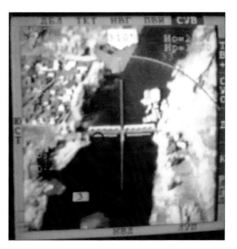

Footage of the Su-30KN launching an R-77...

...and dropping a TV-guided bomb.

Stills from a video showing a 'bomb's eye view' of various targets as seen on the Su-30KN's cockpit displays.

In September 2000 the Su-30KN visited the Ghelendjik-2000 Hydro Aviation Show, arriving from the Russian AF State Flight Test Centre in Akhtoobinsk.

The Su-30KN basks in the sun at Ghelendjik shortly before a demonstration flight.

Three views of the Su-30KN as it completes its landing run at Ghelendjik.

The Su-30KN totes a pair of Kh-31P ARMs, two R-73 AAMs on the wingtip rails and two R-77s (RVV-AEs) under the engine nacelles.

Gear still down, the Su-30KN passes overhead immediately after take-off.

Three views of the Su-30KN tucking up its landing gear and entering a turn to starboard.

Su-30MK demonstrator (the first to have this designation; ex-596 White, c/n 79371010101).

Production Su-30 (c/n 96310107035), Russian Air Force, 148th TsBP i PLS, Savostleyka AB.

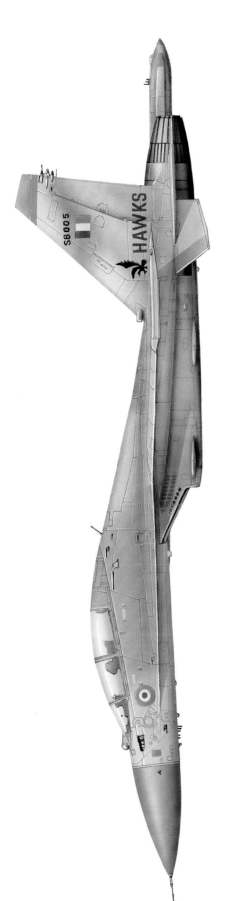

An Indian Air Force Su-30.

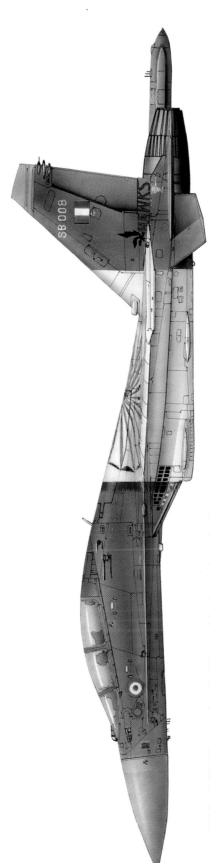

IAF Su-30 SB 008 was painted in this special colour scheme for the Independence Day celebrations.

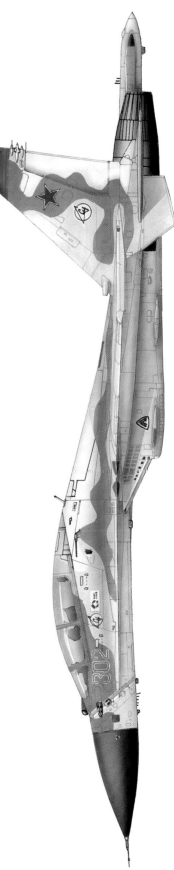

The prototype of the Su-30KN multi-role fighter (c/n 79371010302).

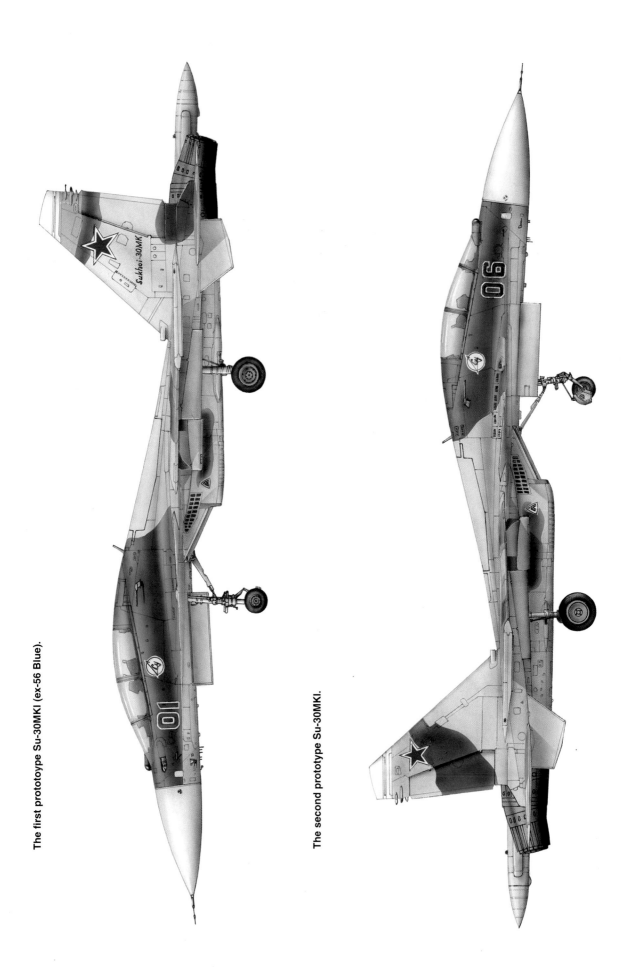

The first prototoype Su-30MKI (ex-56 Blue).

The second prototype Su-30MKI.

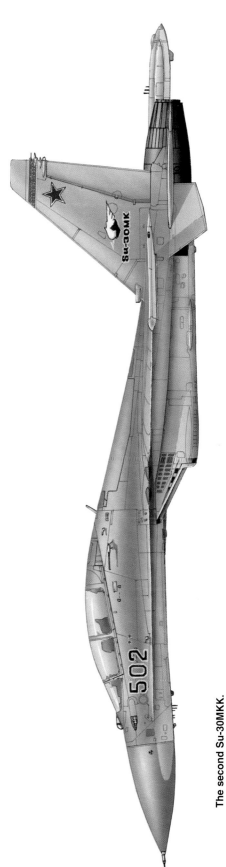

The second Su-30MKK.

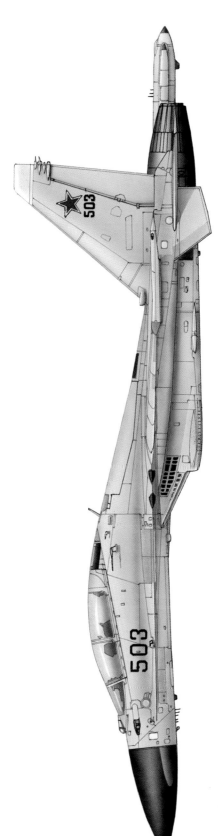

The third Su-30MKK.

The first pre-production Su-30MK.

61

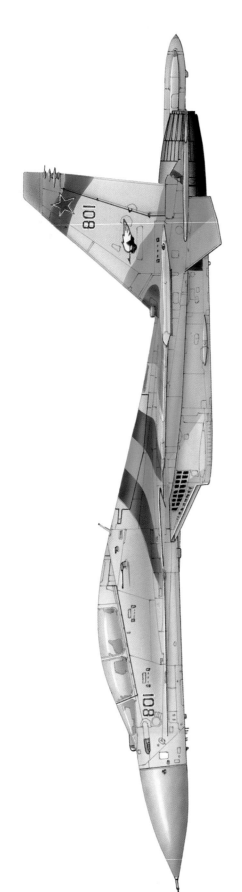

The first prototype Su-35UB.

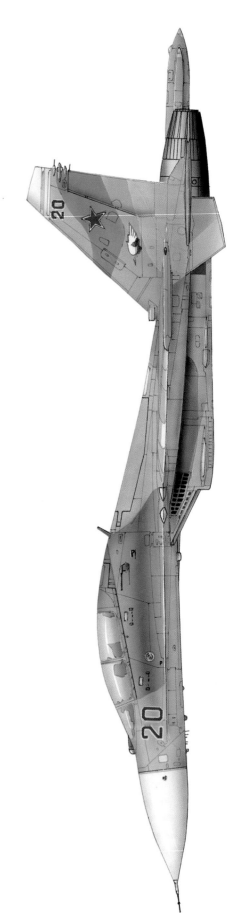

The first Su-27UB to be upgraded to Su-27UBM standard.

At the Ghelendjik-2000 Hydro Aviation Show the Su-30KN made formation flights with the single-seat Su-27PD.

allowing new air-to-air and air-to-surface missiles to be integrated. True, this configuration developed by the Roosskaya Avionika (Russian Avionics) company gives a smaller growth in combat potential than the avionics proposed by RPKB for the Su-30MK. Yet, it is cheaper and, importantly, enables a common equipment standard to be used on Mikoyan and Sukhoi fighters operated by the Russian Air Force.

Speaking of weapons, the Su-30KN can carry up to six Kh-29T AGMs or KAB-500Kr guided bombs, KAB-1500 'smart bombs', two Kh-59M TV-guided cruise missiles and up to six П-77 (ПVV-AE) AAMs. For SEAD missions the aircraft is configured with up to six Kh-31P anti-radiation missiles – or a similar number of Kh-31A ASMs in the anti-shipping strike role. TV-guided weapons can be launched from beyond visual range, since the fighter's radar downloads target data to the weapon's guidance system and the TV seeker head acquires the target as the missile approaches.

The Su-30's counter-air capability is greatly enhanced by merely replacing a single display in each cockpit. The MFI-55 displays flight or tactical information, the pilot selecting display modes at the touch of a button. Installation of just one new display 'per capita' (by comparison, the upgraded MiG-29SMT has three) allows the aircraft to be upgraded quickly and cheaply. Importantly, it also facilitates conversion training; as a rule,

installation of MFDs necessitates a major training programme because data presentation methods are completely different. A single MFD is easier to adapt to, enabling service pilots to quickly master the use of precision weapons against surface targets.

The new equipment increased empty weight by a mere 30 kg (66 lb), which means the fighter's performance is virtually unaffected. Conversely, the combat potential is increased several times, enabling the Su-30KN to rival the USA's currently most potent strike aircraft in front-line service, the Boeing (McDD) F-15E Strike Eagle.

A standard production Su-30 (c/n 79371010302, f/n 03-02) was set aside for conversion as the future Su-30KN prototype, making its first flight in March 1999 at the hands of Anatoliy N. Kvochur. Before the month was out the fighter arrived in Zhukovskiy to undergo manufacturer's flight tests.

Appropriately coded 302 Blue and wearing the Sukhoi and IAPO badges, the still-unpainted (and nameless) aircraft took part in the MAKS-99 airshow (17th-22nd August), carrying dummy Kh-31As and low-drag bombs. Its demonstration flights included a simulated refuelling by an IL-78M tanker (36 Blue, c/n 1013405197, f/n 8010). IAPO spokesman Aleksey Fyodorov stated at the show that Roosskaya Avionika's upgrade concept for the Su-30 has proved viable, passing Stage 1 of the State acceptance

trials at the Russian AF Research Centre in Ahktoobinsk (929th GLITs).

Wearing recently applied three-tone grey/black 'splatter' camouflage reminiscent of that worn a year earlier by the Su-30KI, the Su-30KN prototype took part in the third biennial Hydro Aviation Show held in the Russian Black Sea resort town of Ghelendjik on 6th-10th September 2000. The aircraft arrived at the show directly from Akhtoobinsk where it was then undergoing Stage 2 of the State acceptance trials. Previously (during Stage 1) the fighter successfully launched R-77 (RVV-AE) AAMs and used a wide range of air-to-surface precision weapons. The latter included guided bombs, Kh-29 and Kh-31A ASMs, and Kh-31P ARMs.

According to IAPO Vice-President Mikhail Korzhooyev, 302 Blue has passed a comprehensive trials programme both in Zhukovskiy and in Akhtoobinsk. Interestingly, the programme involved only two-thirds of the originally specified number of test flights – this was enough to achieve the desired results. Also, the Su-30KN met the manufacturer's specifications completely, which is a pretty rare occurrence in Russia; it is all too common for the real aircraft's performance to fall short of expectations.

Russian Air Force Deputy C-in-C (Armament) Lt Gen Yuriy P. Klishin was also satisfied with the Su-30KN's upgraded avionics suite which ensures accurate weapons delivery. There have been reports that

Test pilots Anatoliy N. Kvochur and Aleksandr Yu. Garnayev perform a demonstration flight in the Su-30KN.

unspecified foreign customers are already contemplating the new fighter.

At the show the Su-30KN carried an acquisition round emulating the Kh-59M TV-guided cruise missile on one of the wing pylons. Simulated launches using fixed acquisition rounds are common practice when such extremely expensive precision weapons are tested. Integration of the Kh-59M with the fighter's weapons control system is apparently being done by IAPO jointly with a LII branch named 'Aerobatic Research Centre' State Company which also had a hand in the Su-30KN's development. IAPO are confident that when the aircraft successfully completes its trials programme there will be no obstacles to upgrading operational Flankers to Su-30KN standard. Current plans involve updating a handful of Su-27UBs and Su-30s operated by the Russian Air Force. Retrofitting the Su-30KN's avionics package to single-seat Su-27 Flanker-Bs is also possible but IAPO specialists consider this inadvisable at this stage, as it will excessively increase pilot workload.

As of now, this is just the first stage of the MLU programme. The planned Stage II will give the Su-30KN an avionics suite identical to that of the MiG-29SMT, including a MIL-STD-1553B multiplex databus and two or three 6x8" MFI-68 displays developed by Roosskaya Avionika in each cockpit.

Fyodorov and Korzhooyev regard the Su-30KN mid-life update as the best upgrade option for the Russian Air Force in the current conditions because it does not require extensive and costly changes to the existing avionics suite, including integration of a new fire control radar. Currently Roosskaya Avionika's licence to kill... sorry, to develop military hardware has been suspended; however, the President of IAPO believes this will not affect the Su-30KN programme in any way, since there will always be small but innovative avionics companies capable of a breakthrough in this area which will carry on with the work. (Makes you wonder if Roosskaya Avionika's elimination from the military market was engineered by competitors with some political clout...)

Not to be outdone, Roosskaya Avionika says that its mission avionics enable the Su-30KN to carry heavier weapons than would have been possible with competitors' products. These include the K310MA Yakhont (Emerald/SS-N-26) supersonic anti-shipping missile designed by NPO Mashinostroyeniya in Reutov near Moscow. The missile was displayed alongside the Su-30KN but, unfortunately, was not hooked up to it, and the potential sensation failed to materialise.

Combined with the Su-27/Su-30 family as a weapons platform, the Yakhont ASM forms a weapons system in a class of its own. Among other things, the new missile has twice the range of the Kh-31A and Raduga 3M80 Moskit (Mosquito/SS-N-22 *Sunburn*) ASMs currently on the Russian naval air arm's inventory – 300 km (162 nm) versus 150 km (81 nm). No other aircraft weapons system in the world can boast such an impressive combination of speed, range, warhead power and sophisticated targeting system. Small wonder that foreign delegations at the show were quite interested in the Yakhont. (**Note:** Though primarily surface-to-

surface (shipboard) missiles, as reflected by their NATO code names, the Moskit and Yakhont can be carried on the centreline by the Flanker (notably the Su-27K shipboard fighter). A Ukrainian book mentions the Su-27K as being displayed several times with the Kh-41 anti-shipping missile; this suggests the air-launched version of the Moskit is designated Kh-41.)

IAPO and LII engineers are currently working on more efficient ways of flight data/tactical information presentation. One of the ideas now being implemented is to control the functions of the MFDs by means of a mini-joystick located on the throttles as part of the hands-on-throttle-and-stick (HOTAS) concept. This works better in a combat environment than push-buttons located around the MFD (there's less danger of pushing the wrong button during high-G manoeuvres, for instance). The new cockpit architecture is being tested on LII's Su-30 '597 White' and will probably be unveiled at one of the world's major airshows in the near future.

Still, some industry experts claim that existing versions of the Flanker family have inadequate air-to-surface capability. Hence NPO Mashinostroyeniya is integrating the Alpha anti-shipping missile with the Su-30KN's weapons control system. The Alpha has better growth potential than the 3M80 Moskit and is much more potent than the Kh-31A which is currently Russian tactical aviation's main anti-ship weapon. Outside the CIS, the Su-27 and Su-30 are operated mainly by India, China and Vietnam, all of them marine powers which urgently need aircraft with enhanced anti-ship capabilities.

Chapter 3

Big Head Flankers

Two-seat Strike Aircraft/Tactical Fighter-bombers

By the early 1980s the Soviet Air Force's tactical arm had a requirement for a new-generation multi-role tactical aircraft combining high speed and agility with a big ordnance load and long range. These contradictory demands could only be met by making use of the latest know-how in aerodynamics, manufacturing technologies and other areas of aircraft engineering, as well as integrating new-generation avionics and weapons. The Sukhoi OKB took on this complex task in the mid-1980s shortly after the Su-27 interceptor had entered production; this aircraft was chosen as the starting point.

Developed as a replacement for the ageing Su-24M *Fencer-D* tactical bomber, the new Sukhoi strike aircraft bore the manufacturer's designation T10-V. General Designer Mikhail P. Simonov supervised the programme, while Rolan G. Martirosov was appointed chief project engineer.

Specialist design bureaux were also involved. The mission avionics suite was 'subcontracted' to NPO Leninets (Leninist) in Leningrad led by General Designer G. N. Gromov (aka VNIIRA – *Vsesoyooznyy naoochno-issledovatel'skiy institoot rahdioelektronnovo oboroodovaniya*, All-Union Avionics Research Institute; now the Leninets Holding Company). Three design bureaux – the Vympel MKB under G. A. Sokolovskiy, the Zvezda OKB under G. I. Khokhlov and the Raduga MKB under I. S. Seleznyov – were responsible for the armament.

The T10-V was a rework of the stillborn T10KM-2 naval trainer project (described in the next chapter) and featured the latter's all-new and much wider forward fuselage with side-by-side seating. This arrangement made the aircraft more suitable for the bomber, tanker, recce, ECM and other roles. Unlike the basic Su-27 which had a forward fuselage of basically circular cross-section, the T10-V had a flattened nose with sharp chines reminiscent of the Lockheed SR-71 Blackbird which continued aft until they blended into the LERXes; this promptly gave rise to the nickname *Ootkonos* (platypus).

Accordingly the canopy was redesigned

When the ITAR-TASS news agency published this photo, many people were deluded into thinking the T10-V was a trainer version of the Su-27K and misidentified it as the 'Su-27KU'.

completely and forward fuselage cross-section area was increased. The cockpit was accessed from behind via the nosewheel well by means of a retractable ladder – a feature more commonly found on strategic aircraft. The flight deck roof was aft-hinged but opened only for ejection seat maintenance or removal – or ejection

Sukhoi engineers benefited from operational experience with low-flying attack aircraft when designing the cockpit section. To improve survivability this was a built as a welded capsule of titanium armour up to 17 mm (0.67 in.) thick; live firing trials showed this to adequate. The fuselage fuel tank and the engine nacelles were also armour-protected, increasing survivability during low-level operations over a battlefield saturated with enemy AD systems. Thus the T10-V continued the traditions of the Su-25 *Frogfoot* strike aircraft and the famous Il'yushin Il-2 attack aircraft of the Second World War.

The armour weighed 1,480 kg (3,262 lb), so a new twin-wheel nose gear unit with KN-27 non-braking wheels (tyre size 680x260 mm/26.7x10.2 in.) was designed to absorb the extra weight. Because of the unusual cockpit access arrangement it was moved

Test pilot Yevgeniy Revoonov (left) and test navigator/WSO Yevgeniy Donchenko after a successful flight in the T10V-1.

forward considerably, retracting aft (rather than forward, as on previous Flanker versions). The nosewheel well was closed by two pairs of doors instead of the single side-hinged door found on previous versions.

The forward fuselage terminated in a bay aft of the flight deck which accommodated the greater part of the aircraft's avionics on racks (also accessed via the nosewheel well) and the ammunition box of the internal cannon.

Top, above and left: Three views of the T10V-1 at LII's airfield in Zhukovskiy.

Top and above: The T10V-1 basks in the sun in front of the Sukhoi hangar in Zhukovskiy.

Unlike subsequent T10-Vs, the first prototype had single-wheel main gear units.

Above and opposite page: The second prototype (T10V-2) on a snow-covered hardstand at LII.

The T10V-2 with a full ordnance load. Note the white-painted Alpha anti-shipping missile on the starboard inboard wing station.

Outwardly the T10V-2 differed from the T10B-1 in having twin-wheel main gear bogies and a longer and fatter tail 'stinger'.

Above left and right: Production Su-34s during final assembly at NAPO.

An air-to-air of the T10V-1 during a test flight.

The T10V-1 was shown with a full weapons load at Machoolischchi AB on 13th February 1992.

To improve agility and field performance the T10-V featured canards, which meant the LERXes had to be extended forward. The fully-adjustable supersonic air intakes of the fighter version gave way to simple fixed-area intakes, since high-altitude performance is not so important for a tactical bomber flying mostly at low altitude and festooned with draggy external stores. (The fixed-area intakes impaired performance slightly, especially maximum Mach number, but saved weight.) The ventral fins were deleted for much the same reasons. The wings and vertical tails were reinforced. The AL-31F engines were replaced by AL-31FMs uprated to 12,800 kgp (28,218 lb st) in full afterburner and featuring full authority digital engine control (FADEC), and the number of hardpoints was increased to 12.

The fuel system comprised four integral fuel tanks – three in the fuselage and one in the wings (divided into two sections, one per outer wing). Fuel capacity was increased as compared to the Su-27/Su-30. Additionally, two of the wing pylons were 'wet', permitting carriage of drop tanks. There was also a retractable IFR probe ahead of the windscreen offset to port (identical to that of the Su-27K (Su-33), Su-30 and Su-27M (Su-35) enabling it to take on fuel from IL-78 tankers or other aircraft fitted with UPAZ-1A standardised refuelling pods.

The first prototype, T10V-1 (42 Blue), was converted from a standard Su-27UB in Novosibirsk. A new nose section was manufactured by NAPO and mated to a 'chopped-up' trainer airframe. It should be noted that NAPO is a long-standing Sukhoi partner. Factory No. 153 had built the Su-15 *Flagon* interceptor – and the Su-24, so the choice of this factory to build a follow-on to the *Fencer* was hardly a matter of chance.

Defying superstition, the T10V-1 made its first flight in Zhukovskiy on 13th April 1990 at the hands of Distinguished test pilot Anatoliy

The Su-32FN (T10V-5) takes off from Kubinka AB.

Ivanov, one of the company's best pilots. The manufacturer's flight test programme continued well into 1991. Later the first prototype was officially designated Su-27IB, the suffix letters denoting *istrebitel'-bombardirovschchik* (fighter-bomber).

The OKB built numerous test rigs to verify the Su-27IB's new systems. One rig featured a full-scale Flanker airframe incorporating a retractable brake parachute container, with powerful fans placed in front of it to simulate the slipstream. This was because the T10-V's tail 'stinger' would house a rear warning radar, which required the brake 'chute to be relocated. Special attention was paid to the crew escape system which was tested on a forward fuselage attached to a rocket-powered sled. Ejection time was cut by nearly two-thirds as compared to the Su-24M; still, the rescue system took a lot of debugging which continued even as the aircraft entered flight tests.

The Su-27IB was officially unveiled at Machoolischchi AB near Minsk on 13th February 1992 when the latest military aircraft were displayed to the leaders of the CIS states (including Russian President Boris Yel'tsin) holding a summit in the Belorussian capital. The idea of this exclusive display was to impress the President and talk him into securing additional funds for R&D programmes so that further prototypes could be built. Attending MoD and MAP officials were hoping for new orders from the CIS Air Force which would pave the way for full-scale production of new aircraft – including the Su-27IB.

Interestingly, the data plates in front of the numerous aircraft on show were carefully draped with black cloth and unwrapped only for the VIPs. Military personnel on site did their utmost to make sure that the prying journalists (who arrived in force) did not see the 'top secret' performance figures. Obviously *glasnost* still had a long way to go in 1992!

The T10V-1 with IFR probe extended, seen from an IL-78 tanker during a test flight.

However, news of the *Ootkonos* had leaked to the popular press (and hence to the West) a while earlier. In mid-1990 the Su-27IB deployed briefly to the AVMF Flight Test Centre at Novofyodorovka AB in Saki on the Crimea Peninsula. This may seem strange, since the Su-27IB is not a naval aircraft. The reason, however, was simple enough: Soviet President Mikhail S. Gorbachov, who was vacationing in the Crimea, wished to inspect the new military hardware taking part in a Black Sea Fleet exercise. Among other things he visited the aircraft carrier SNS (Soviet Navy ship) *Tbilisi* which was undergoing post-modification seagoing trials at the time.

Three Su-27K prototypes were operating from the *Tbilisi* at the time, and Sukhoi OKB leaders decided to demonstrate the latest spinoff of the Su-27 to the President for good measure. Sukhoi test pilots made an impressive simulated carrier approach. However, whether by chance or not, A. Kremko, a correspondent of the TASS information agency, was aboard the carrier that very day and photographed the Su-27IB as it came in. This first official photo was promptly circulated by TASS under the rather incongruous caption 'Landing on the aircraft-carrying cruiser *Tbilisi*' – even though an arrestor hook was nowhere to be seen.

Western intelligence agencies swallowed the bait and labelled the aircraft 'Su-27KU' (probably having got wind of that project somehow). Thus the West was deluded into thinking Sukhoi were testing a naval trainer to complement the Su-27K – which of course was good for the OKB (and the KGB). However, it was the same TASS information agency that terminally spilled the beans by publishing photos of 42 Blue taken at

This page and opposite page (top and centre): Five views of the T10V-5 (Su-34, aka Su-32FN)

The T10V-5 (Su-34/Su-32FN) on LII's runway.

The Su-34 (Su-32FN) with an impressive load of dummy missiles during a test flight.

The T10V-2 (in the background) shares the Sukhoi hangar with the T10V-5 which is pushed back into the hangar after a test flight.

The Su-34 had its service debut in 2000, taking part in a Russian Air Force exercise.

The Su-34's nose gear unit and boarding ladder

The Su-34's main gear units

The Su-34 had the same blended wing/body (BWB) layout as the rest of the Flanker family. The use of advanced structural materials such as composites and titanium, together with the absence of the Su-24's variable-geometry wings and associated heavy wing joints/actuators, gave the Su-34 a higher payload, longer range and better field performance as compared to its predecessor.

Outwardly the Su-34 differed little from the Su-27IB prototype, the most obvious external difference being the landing gear design. To cater for the higher gross weight the single large mainwheels borrowed straight from a standard Flanker were replaced by twin-71wheel bogies. This was probably designed to give the Su-34 soft-field capability, allowing it to operate from unpaved tactical airstrips.

The relatively small but wide KT-206 mainwheels (tyre size 950x400 mm/ 37.4x15.7 in.) were located in tandem *a la* SAAB JA-37 Viggen, spreading the load over a bigger area. This was particularly important when landing with a partially used (or rather partially unused!) weapons load and permitted operations from unprepared tactical airstrips, albeit at a reduced MTOW. The bogies rotated 90° nose-up before retraction to lie horizontally in the wing roots with the rear wheels foremost, folding into a remarkably small space. (The main gear underwent a similar evolution on the MiG-31 as compared to the MiG-25P *Foxbat* from which it was developed, but the MiG-31 has a unique staggered-tandem arrangement.)

The tail 'stinger' was much longer and fatter than the Su-27IB's, accommodating additional fuel. It terminated in a large dielectric fairing, plainly indicating that the Su-34 had provision for a rear warning radar (probably the NIIP N-012). Apart from the warning function, the radar could guide AAMs (including the R-77/RVV-AE) capable of destroying not only aircraft but guided missiles as well – a feature not currently found on any Western strike aircraft. Installation of the radar meant that the brake parachute container had to be moved forward (as had been the case with the Su-35/Su-37); it popped up like a jack-in-the-box when the parachute was deployed.

Crew fatigue during long sorties is a constant problem, and Sukhoi have gone to great lengths to fix it. The Su-34 is unique among tactical fighter-bombers as regards crew comfort. 'Cockpit' is hardly the word to describe the crew quarters: it is really a flight deck worthy of a much larger aircraft. Indeed, when the Su-27IB was demonstrated to Air Force and Navy commanders, VVS C-in-C Col Gen Pyotr S. Deynekin remarked: 'It has a bigger cockpit than the Tu-160!' (This is more than a joke: *Blackjack* crews keep complaining about their cramped and inconvenient workstations.)

To take crew comfort a little bit further NPP Zvezda (*na**ooch**no-proiz**vod**stvennoye*

Machoolischchi; the aircraft was bristling with air-to-ground missiles, which left no doubts as to its true role.

Later the Su-27IB was demonstrated to the general public at MosAeroShow '92 and MAKS-93 with Distinguished test pilot Yevgeniy Revoonov and test navigator (2nd class) Yevgeniy Donchenko. On the first occasion the aircraft hooked up to the prototype IL-78M tanker (CCCP-76701), formating with the Su-27PD and a Su-30 from Anatoliy Kvochur's aerobatic team in a simulated three-ship refuelling. Immediately afterwards the Su-27IB gave a brief aerobatics display, demonstrating excellent handling. Photos published after the show gave Western experts a fairly good idea of the aircraft's capabilities.

The second prototype (T10V-2) was the first of several pre-production examples built

in Novosibirsk from beginning to end. Coded 43 Blue and wearing a three-tone blue/grey camouflage, it was also the first Su-27IB in production configuration. The latter incorporated enough changes to warrant a new service designation, Su-34 (probably chosen to stress the 'father and son' relationship with the Su-24).

The aircraft was designed to destroy small heavily-protected ground targets in any weather, day and night. As a shore-based maritime strike/anti-submarine warfare (ASW) aircraft, it was to seek, identify and destroy surface ships and submarines in an active ECM environment. To this end the Su-34 was equipped with state-of-the-art mission avionics, including the V-004 high-resolution multi-mode fire control radar developed by the Leninets Holding Company for pinpoint strikes.

predpriyahtiye – Scientific and Production Enterprise, aka OKB-918; not to be confused with the aforementioned weapons design bureau) based in Lyubedrtsy near Moscow and headed by Guy Il'yich Severin developed a version of the famous K-36DM ejection seat with a built-in back massage function! A galley and a toilet are located in a compartment aft of the crew seats. The flight deck is spacious enough to walk around in without stooping – or even stretch out on the floor between the seats (one at a time) if fatigue really gets you! As on the Su-27IB, a powerful air conditioning system automatically maintains air pressure corresponding to 2,400 m (7,874 ft) at flight levels up to 10,000 m (32,808 ft), enabling the crew to work without using oxygen masks. Thus, mission time can be extended to ten hours, boosting the Su-34's combat potential considerably.

The bay aft of the flight deck houses most of the avionics and the ammunition box of the internal cannon (hence the T10-V's characteristic 'hump'). Integral fuel tanks filled with explosion-suppression foam occupy the centre fuselage. Two hardpoints for anti-shipping missiles (on the naval version) or other heavy air-to-surface weapons are located in tandem on the fuselage centreline.

Like the Su-35 fighter, the Su-34 has digital FBW controls. However, it also has an active flight safety system (AFSS). The latter has pitch stabilisation and terrain following functions, enabling the aircraft to manoeuvre sharply at its maximum sea level speed of 1,380 km/h (766 kts) and assisting in penetrating enemy air defences. There is also a 'panic button' function: the pilot can bring the aircraft into straight and level flight from any attitude by pushing a button on the stick (eg, in the event of disorientation). The AFSS incorporates artificial intelligence, automatically monitoring the pilots' physical condition, systems status and fuel quantity; it even enables automatic return to base and runway approach, should the pilot be disabled.

The canards, together with the pitch stabilisation feature and the flight control system's state-of-the-art computers, considerably enhance manoeuvrability at low altitude, giving the Su-34 a smooth ride in turbulence. This enables the crew to operate more efficiently when it comes to delivering weapons and avoiding hostile fire.

Like the Su-27IB prototype, the Su-34 is fitted with a retractable refuelling probe. A Su-24M or another Su-34 fitted with an UPAZ-1A 'buddy' refuelling pod can act as a tanker. Thanks to the large internal fuel volume and provision for drop tanks the aircraft has an unrefuelled range of 4,000 km (2,222 nm). With a single top-up, range increases to 7,000 km (3,888 nm), approaching that of medium bombers – the Tu-16 *Badger*, Tu-22 *Blinder* and Tu-22M *Backfire*; the fuel-efficient turbofans and excellent aerodynamics

The crew makes the final cockpit check before a test flight.

The cockpit canopy of the Su-34 (Su-32FN)

The forward fuselage of the T10V-2

The pilots make a walk-around before a flight.

also contribute to this. In a nutshell, the Su-34 is better suited for quick deployment to remote bases than most strike aircraft.

The airframe makes use of stealth technology. As already mentioned, the radome has sharp chines blending into the LERXes; together with the BWB layout, this reduces the aircraft's RCS while ensuring good aerodynamics. Stealth is further helped by radar-absorbent coatings and the absence of ventral fins. The Su-34 has a much lower RCS than other aircraft in the same class (the Su-24, General Dynamics F-111 and McDD F-15E); Sukhoi claim that in low-level flight the RCS is comparable to that of a modern cruise missile.

Survivability is not concerned with armour alone. The Su-34 has dual controls, enabling the WSO/navigator to take over if the pilot is disabled, and the avionics are triply redundant to increase reliability.

Speaking of avionics, the aircraft is equipped with a completely new computerised navigation suite which can be programmed to guide the Su-34 automatically to a given location with an error margin of 1 m (3 ft). The navigation suite includes an INS, radio navigation aids and GPS.

The flight deck features multi-mode colour LCD displays, as well as two HUDs. In addition, the pilot and navigator have helmet-mounted sights for use with 'point and shoot' weapons such as the Kh-29T TV-guided AGM. The HMS dramatically reduces targeting time, which is especially important during low-level sorties when the pilot has only a few seconds in which to spot the target, identify it and take aim. The radar is capable of detecting aerial targets, including small ones, up to

250 km (138 nm) away.

Sukhoi OKB General Designer Mikhail P. Simonov states that the Su-34 also has considerable potential as a maritime strike/ASW aircraft. Its avionics suite enables it to hunt subs and surface ships, detect minefields and perform maritime reconnaissance. The V-004 multi-mode coherent pulse-Doppler radar is guaranteed to detect surface ships within a 3,000-m² (32,258-sq. ft) RCS and is able to spot the wake of a submarine at 150 km (83 nm) when the aircraft is flying high. The avionics suite renders the Su-34 suitable for peaceful tasks such as search and rescue (SAR) and marine ecological survey.

The mission avionics suite has an increased data processing capability. The Argon mainframe computer is linked to specially programmed additional processors by multiplex databuses. It co-ordinates all avionics operation, taking care of data exchange, and feeds target and systems information to the crew during the sortie. According to project chief Rolan G. Martirosov, the computer's modular construction and hardware/software duplication increases reliability, which means the mission will be accomplished even if some of the processors fail.

Both hardware and software are duplicated for greater reliability, so that the mission can be accomplished even if some of the processors fail. The modular structure allows the avionics suite to be configured to fit customer requirements; Western avionics may be used for export aircraft.

Part of the mission avionics (eg, thermal imaging equipment or TV target designators for AGMs and guided bombs) will probably be podded so that the aircraft can be easily configured for a specific mission.

In maritime patrol/ASW configuration the Su-34 relies mainly on radar and sonobuoys, as well as forward-looking infra-red (FLIR) and laser ranging equipment. Low light level TV systems may also be used. For ASW duties the aircraft carries up to 72 active and passive sonobuoys operating within a broad spectrum of frequencies, as well as explosive sound sources (small bombs which detonate at a preset depth, generating sound waves assisting in tracking the sub). Sukhoi claim that the sonobuoys compatible with the Su-34 are more capable than the SSQ-53B, SSQ-75 and SSQ-77A buoys used by the US Navy.

Additionally, the naval version is to be fitted with a magnetic anomaly detector (MAD) in the tail 'stinger' used in conjunction with the sonobuoys for submarine detection. The radar detects small targets such as periscopes and monitors sonobuoy operation. The pilots will be equipped with the VMSK naval heat-insulated pressure/rescue suit (*vysotnyy morskoy spasahtel'nyy kostyum*) saving them from hypothermia in the event of ejection over the sea.

Mikhail P. Simonov claims that the V-004 radar has 25 to 30% better performance than its US counterpart, the AN/APS-137. The Su-34's capabilities are enhanced by the use of FLIR and LLLTV which may be used separately or together, depending on the weather conditions and time of day.

The built-in electronic intelligence (ELINT) system is in standby mode most of the time. After detecting signals indicating the presence of a submarine in the search area or beyond the horizon it identifies the source of the signal and gives a bearing on it. The ESM suite may include ELINT and ECM pods, an infra-red missile warning system (MWS) detecting incoming missiles by their heat signature.

The aircraft can carry two NPO Mashinostroyeniya 3M80 Moskit (ASM-MSS; NATO SS-N-22 *Sunburn*) anti-shipping missiles instead of one. The missile weighs 4,000 kg (8,818 lb) and travels 250 km (138 nm) at Mach 3.0. Alternatively, the Su-34 can be armed with three NPO Mashinostroyeniya Alpha (AFM-L) ASMs; the 1,500-kg (3,306-lb) Alpha has a range of 300 km (166 nm) and a cruising speed of Mach 2.2 to 3.0.

Of course, the Su-34 can also carry ordinary 'dumb bombs' weighing from 100 to 500 kg (220 to 1,102 lb), KMGU submunitions pods (*kont**ey**ner dlya **mah**logabari**t**nykh **groo**zov ooniver**sahl**'nyy* – versatile small items container, typically loaded with anti-tank or anti-personnel mines) and unguided rockets. The latter include B-8M pods with twenty 80-mm (3.15-in.) S-8 folding-fin aircraft rockets (FFARs) each, UB-13 missile pods with five 122-mm (4.8-in.) S-13 FFARs each and 266-mm (10.47-in.) S-25 rockets on O-25 disposable launchers. The same unguided weapons are carried by other strike-capable versions of the Flanker (Su-27SK/ SMK, Su-35 and Su-30MK). The maximum ordnance load is 8,000 kg (17,636 lb).

In comparison with the Su-24M the new bomber has not just a bigger ordnance load (8,000 kg/17,636 lb) but also a bigger array of weapons usable at 250 km (135 nm) range. For air-to-air engagements the Su-34 is armed with a 30-mm GSh-301 cannon, R-77 (RVV-AE) medium-range missiles and R-73 short-range AAMs. It can also carry guided bombs. If surface ships are the target, all targeting systems are brought into play to ensure target lock-on at maximum range. This, and the long-range missiles, allows the Su-34 to stay beyond the reach of the ship's air defence systems.

The Su-34 is heavier than the pure fighter versions of the Flanker (MTOW is 45,000 kg/99,206 lb and normal TOW is 42,000 kg/92,592 lb), yet performance has deteriorated only slightly in comparison with the Su-27 and Su-30. As for the fighter versions, never-exceed speed is 1,400 km/h (777 kts) at sea level and Mach 1.8 at high altitude.

The first flight of 43 Blue on 18th December 1993 was fairly long, lasting 52 minutes. The aircraft was flown by Sukhoi OKB crew (pilot Igor' V. Votintsev and WSO Yevgeniy G. Revoonov). A Su-24 flown by NAPO test pilots Yevgeniy N. Roodakas and A. I. Gaivoronskiy acted as chase plane. On 3rd March 1994 the T10V-2 arrived at LII, Zhukovskiy, after a non-stop ferry flight from Novosibirsk with Ye. Revoonov and Igor' Ye. Solov'yov at the controls.

The second prototype Su-34 (T10V-5), still painted in chrome yellow primer, took off from the factory airfield in Novosibirsk on 28th December 1994 – almost exactly a year after the T10V-2's first flight. The aircraft was flown by Ye. Roodakas and Ye. Revoonov. This was in effect the first production Su-34. In keeping with tradition, a Su-24 flown by I. Solov'yov and R. Asadoolin flew as chase plane.

In the first days of June 1995, the T10V-5 arrived at LII for a 'brush-up' prior to its international debut at the 41st Paris Air Show. Wearing a rather shocking iridescent green/blue camouflage and the low-visibility tactical code 45 White outline, it was demonstrated to Mikhail Simonov and a group of officials a few days before departing to Paris. However, the demo – the aircraft's 18th flight – nearly ended in disaster, as the main gear units would not extend at the end of the flight. Luckily the pilots, Igor' Votintsev and Igor' Solov'yov, were quick to realise what had happened; they made a steep left turn over the runway and the G force wrenched the landing gear loose. The aircraft landed with parts of the main gear dangling from the wheel wells, to the immense relief of the spectators, not to mention the crew.

Spares were rushed from Novosibirsk to replace the damaged components, and after hasty repairs the T10V-5 flew to Le Bourget, wearing the exhibit code 349. Interestingly, the data plate in front of the aircraft at the show read 'Su-32FN' (Fighter, Navy), which is apparently the type's export designation. Sukhoi chose to keep the aircraft in the static park throughout the show – quite wisely, as it turned out. More malfunctions came on the return trip (this time in a different system), forcing the aircraft to make an unscheduled stop in Prague.

On 22nd-27th August 1995 the T10V-5 was displayed at the MAKS-95 airshow – once again only in the static park. Some of the visitors dubbed it, rather unkindly, Greenbottle Fly, referring to the garish bright green colour scheme. (This camouflage appears to have been selected for the naval version, being more effective over water.)

The third Su-34 to fly – the T10V-4 (c/n 41606627000573) – was completed almost exactly two years after the second one; strangely enough, the fourth development aircraft came after the fifth one. (The T10V-3

The T10V-5 with the radome removed; the phased array of the Leninets V-004 fire control radar is clearly visible.

This model of the Su-32FN with Sorbtsiya wingtip ECM pods and four supersonic anti-shipping missiles of an unspecified type was displayed at the MAKS-99 airshow.

The K310MA, the air-launched version of the Yakhont (Emerald) ASM, beside the T10V-2 at MAKS-99.

was probably a static test airframe. The c/n is deciphered as follows. '416' is a code for NAPO obtained by manipulating with the factory number (153). '066' means *izdeliye* 66, an in-house code for the Su-34. '27' means the aircraft was released from the factory in the 2nd quarter of 1997. The rest has no meaning whatever so that the c/n would not reveal the batch number/number of the aircraft in the batch and hence how many have been built.) The aircraft flew on 25th December 1996 (once again in primer finish). During the 46-minute first flight which went

smoothly, test pilots Igor' Solov'yov (Sukhoi OKB) and Yevgeniy Roodakas (NAPO) checked the aircraft's handling and systems operation. Unlike previous aircraft, the T10V-4 had a complete avionics fit (developed by the Leninets Holding Company) and was thus the first Su-34 in representative production configuration.

Coded 44 White outline and again wearing the 'Greenbottle Fly' camouflage, the T10V-4 commenced manufacturer's flight test in early 1997. In June 1997 it was displayed at the 42nd Paris Air Show with the exhibit

This sequence shows the T10V-5 taking off on a demonstration flight at MAKS-99. Note how the main gear bogies rotate prior to retraction.

The T10V-5 makes a tight turn to starboard (above) and port (below).

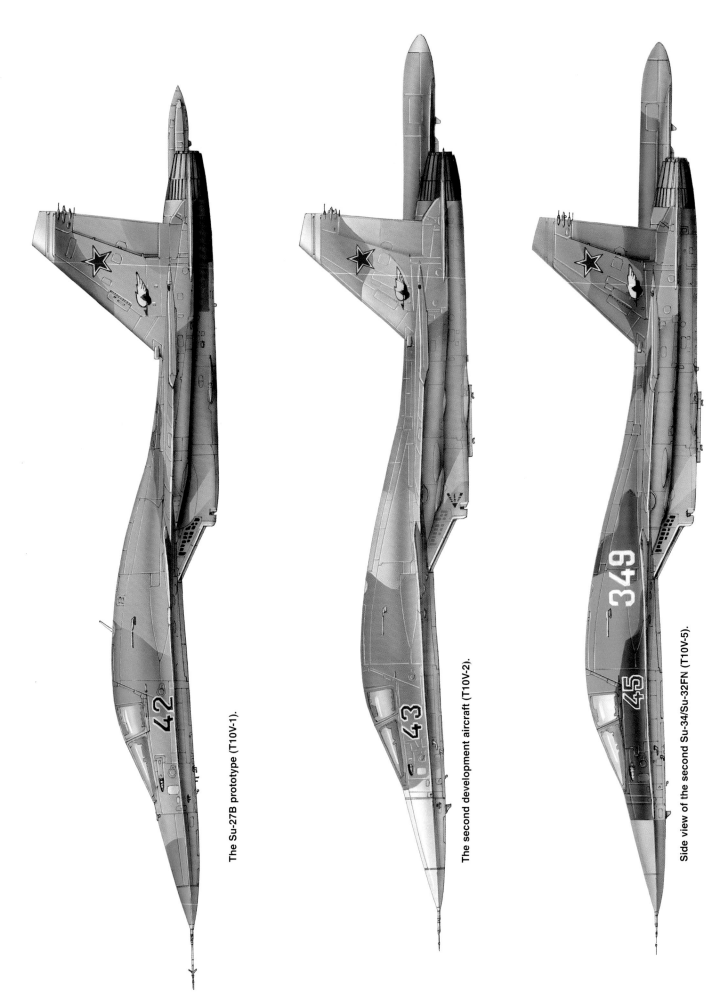

The Su-27B prototype (T10V-1).

The second development aircraft (T10V-2).

Side view of the second Su-34/Su-32FN (T10V-5).

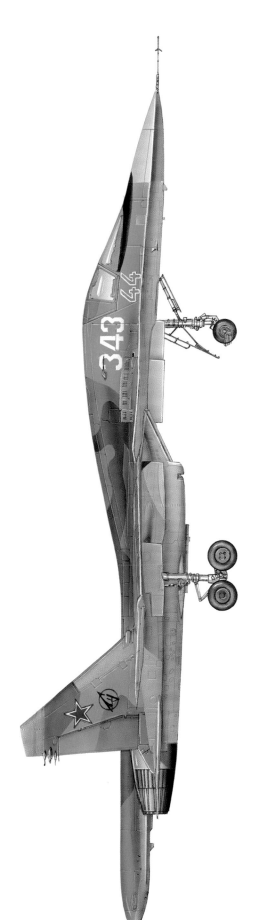

Starboard view of the T10V-4 (Su-34/Su-32 FN, c/n 41606627000573).

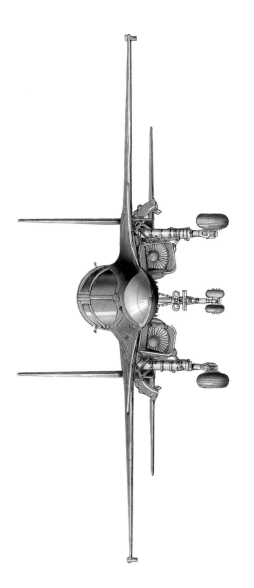

Front view of the T10V-5 (Su-34/Su-32FN).

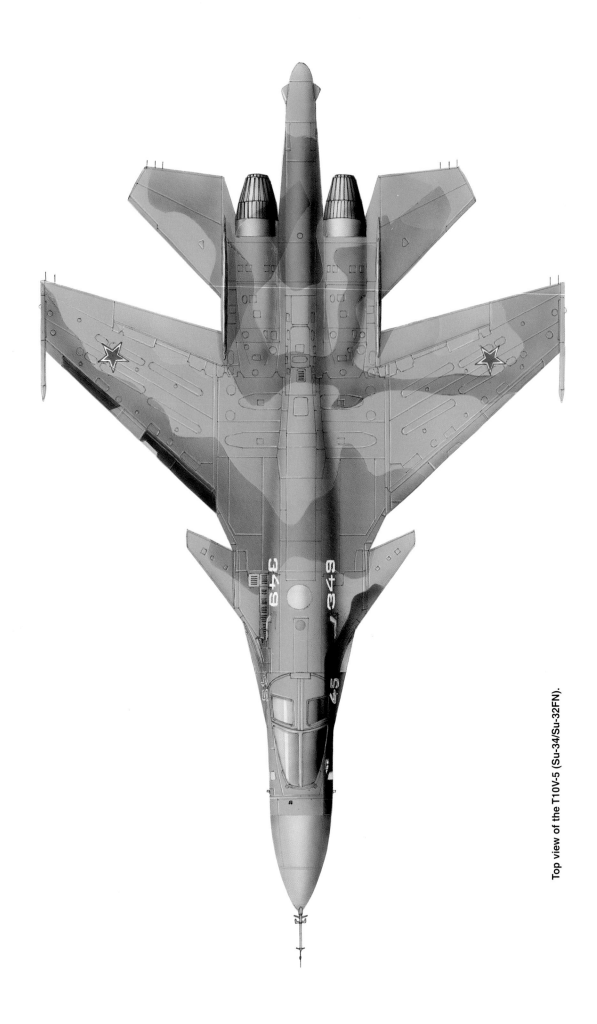

Top view of the T10V-5 (Su-34/Su-32FN).

Bottom view of the T10V-5 (Su-34/Su-32FN).

code 343. This time the Su-34 (displayed as Su-32FN) made several flights at Le Bourget with Igor' Votintsev at the controls, demonstrating excellent agility.

On August 8 the aircraft participated in an air fest held at Kubinka AB to celebrate the 50th anniversary of the 16th Air Army. Eleven days later the T10V-4 was displayed at the MAKS-97 airshow in Zhukovskiy (19th-24th August) with Kh-31P anti-radiation missiles, also participating in the flying display. This indicated clearly that the Su-34 can be used in the 'Wild Weasel' role as well. Sukhoi's display stand at the show featured a model of a Su-34 coded 45 Black outline (?!) and equipped with Sorbtsiya ECM pods replacing the wingtip launch rails for R-73 AAMs (as sometimes fitted to the Su-27 and Su-27K).

The fourth example, the T10V-6 – yet another 'Greenbottle Fly' coded 46 White outline – was completed in 1997. Unfortunately the first flight date and other details are unknown.

Meanwhile, the static test programme was completed in November 1995. Currently Su-34 trials are continuing in low key, with Votintsev, Revoonov and Solovyov as project test pilots; there is no need to hold a full trials programme because of the high degree of commonality with the basic Su-27.

The 60th anniversary of the Sukhoi Design Bureau was duly celebrated with a string of new world records (see table). These were established in Akhtoobinsk by company and Russian Air Force test pilots flying the Su-34. The first records were set by Sukhoi chief test pilot Igor' Votintsev and WSO Aleksandr Gaivoronskiy on 28th July 1999. The aircraft's TOW was 36,160 kg (79,717 lb), including 5,129 kg (11,307 lb) of ordnance. The crew also set three time-to-height world records on the same flight.

Two more records were established on 3rd August by a 929th GLITs crew – pilot Col Vyacheslav Petroosha and WSO Aleksandr Oschchepkov. This time the Su-34 grossed at 34,130 kg (75,242 lb) and reached 15,050 m (49,376 ft) with a 5,000-kg (11,022-lb) payload. Additionally the pilots took a payload of 5,129 kg to an altitude of 2,000 m (6,561 ft).

On 19th August the Platypus excelled again during the MAKS-99 airshow (19th August was the 'Sukhoi day' of the show when the company held its press conference). In the middle of the flying display the second prototype Su-34 (T10V-5) took off to set another three world records. One of them was recorded as follows: a 2,300-kg (5,070-lb) payload taken to an altitude of 16,150 m (52,985 ft). No aircraft in the 35 to 45-ton (77,160 to 99,206-lb) TOW class had ever reached this altitude before.

Interestingly, the record-breaking flight was performed by pilot Igor' Ye. Solov'yov and WSO Vladimir G. Shendrik. Solov'yov

was the son of another Sukhoi test pilot – Gen Yevgeniy Solov'yov who was killed on 7th May 1978 in the crash of the T10-2 Flanker-A, a predecessor of the very aircraft in which Igor' was now setting world records. The first Su-34, 43 Blue, was also present at MAKS-99, being part of the static display.

In 2000 the Su-34 had its operational debut, taking part in a Russian Air Force exercise and confirming its high capabilities. So far the Platypus has not seen actual combat: despite allegations in the press, the type was not used operationally in Chechnya.

In the late 1990s a Russian aviation magazine reported that NAPO had manufactured seven Su-34s (Su-32FNs) by the time of closing for press. The report contained a piece of sensational news: the Sukhoi OKB may fit production aircraft (which are to be delivered to the Russian Air Force from 2002 onwards) with NPO Lyul'ka-Saturn's latest product – the AL-41F new-generation afterburning turbofan rated at approximately 17,700 kgp (39,020 lb st) in full afterburner. (The exact figures are still classified as of this writing.) Originally designed for Mikoyan's as-yet unbuilt fifth-generation fighter, the AL-41F features an axisymmetrical convergent-divergent thrust-vectoring nozzle.

Changes to the avionics suite are also coming. Some sources indicate that the V-004 radar has disappointing performance and the military tasked the Leninets Holding Company with developing a replacement radar. This is reportedly undergoing trials since late 2000 on the company's Tupolev Tu-134SL avionics testbed, CCCP-65098 – a converted Tu-134Sh-1 navigator trainer (c/n 73550845; f/n 0805?) currently fitted with a Su-34 nose replacing the previous Su-27 nose.

If, despite Russia's current economic plight, funding of the Su-34 programme continues, at the turn of the century the Russian Air Force will get a very capable combat aircraft to defend the country's land and maritime borders more efficiently and at lower cost. The Su-34 (Su-32FN) also has considerable export potential.

On 24th-30th July 2000 Su-34 '45 White outline' was displayed at the Farnborough International 2000 airshow where it arrived using the callsign RA-36845 (and still wearing the Le Bourget exhibit code 349). This was the type's first visit to the UK. The aircraft was one of only two Russian aircraft on display at FI'2000, the other one being the latest and as-yet unnamed version of the ubiquitous Mil' Mi-8 *Hip* helicopter. The latter remained firmly on the ground for most of the show; hence the T10V-5 had to save the day, making daily demo flights at the hands of Igor' Votintsev and Igor' Solov'yov.

There was also a sensation: Mikhail A. Pogosyan announced at a press conference that the Russian government had cleared the Su-34/Su-32FN for export in its current configuration and export deliveries could begin in 2002. He declined to state an approximate price, saying it would have to be negotiated specifically with each customer; however, he did say that the Su-34/Su-32FN would not be priced much higher than the Su-30MK in order to make it attractive. Pogosyan remarked that, while the Su-34/Su-32FN was not designed with ultra-manoeuvrability in mind, it was one of the most agile aircraft in its class. Chief project engineer Rolan G. Martirosov added that it would be marketed as a land-based multi-mission day/night strike aircraft capable of destroying ground targets and surface ships; ASW capability would be added later on.

The Su-27IB development aircraft and the Su-34 (Su-32FN) were not allocated a separate NATO reporting name.

World records held by the Su-34 (Su-32FN)

Crew	Date	Record	Class	Value
I. V. Votintsev A. I. Gaivoronskiy	28.07.1999	Altitude with a 5,000-kg (11,022-lb) payload	C, C-1i	14,727 m (48,316 ft)
	28.07.1999	Payload taken to 2,000 m (6,561 ft)	C, C-1i	5,130 kg (11,309 lb)
V. S. Petroosha A. A. Oschchepkov	03.08 1999	Altitude with a 5,000-kg (11,022-lb) payload	C, C-1к	15,063 m (49,419 ft)
	03.08 1999	Payload taken to 15,000 m (49,212 ft)	C, C-1к	5,130 kg (11,309 lb)
I. Ye. Solov'yov V. G. Shendrik	19.08 1999	Altitude with a 1,000-kg (2,204-lb) payload	C, C-1i	16,206 m (53,169 ft)
	19.08 1999	Altitude with a 2,000-kg (4,409-lb) payload	C, C-1i	16,206 m (53,169 ft)
	19.08 1999	Payload taken to 15,000 m (49,212 ft)	C, C-1i	2,330 kg (5,136 lb)

Chapter 4

Out over the Briny

Shipboard Fighters

The obvious necessity to enhance the Soviet Navy's potential with an aircraft carrier led the Ministry of Shipbuilding to task one of its divisions, the Neva Design Bureau in Leningrad (NPKB – **Nev**skoye pro**yekt**no-kon**strook**torskoye byu**ro**), with developing a conventional take-off and landing (CTOL) carrier. Initial research and feasibility studies were made as early as in 1968; however, the project was not included in the military ship-building plan for 1971-1980 because CTOL shipboard aircraft projects on hand were still at a very early development stage.

Yet the SOR for the carrier was beginning to take shape. The 40,000 to 45,000-ton displacement and the carrier wing consisting of 28 fighters and four helicopters outlined in the original project of 1968 were deemed to be insufficient; therefore, in 1972 the NPKB submitted a revised project. The carrier wing now consisted of navalised MiG-23ML *Flogger-G* fighters (featuring an arrestor hook, a beefed-up landing gear and an uprated R-100 turbojet), navalized Su-25K *Frogfoot-A* ground attack aircraft and Beriyev P-42 Garpoon (Harpoon) ASW aircraft; the latter was a chubby straight-wing aircraft powered by two Lotarev D-36 turbofans which bore a striking resemblance to the Lockheed S-3 Viking. (Of these, only the second aircraft was to materialise as the Su-25UTG – *oocheb*no-treni**rov**ochnyy s **gah**kom, arrestor hook-equipped trainer.) This was the first time the Mikoyan, Sukhoi and Beriyev bureaux established direct links with the Ministry of Shipbuilding in order to jointly prepare SORs for the shipboard aircraft.

Having reviewed the project, the Minister of Aircraft Industry, the Minister of Shipbuilding, the Air Force C-in-C and the Navy C-in-C submitted a joint report to the Central Committee of the Communist Party and the MoD in mid-1973, recommending that a nuclear-powered multi-role carrier displacing 80,000 tons be proceeded with. Besides missiles, the carrier was to be equipped with P-42 ASW aircraft and Sukhoi T10-K fighters. This was the manufacturer's designation of the proposed navalised Flanker, the K denot-

ing *korabel'nyy* (shipboard). However, a go-ahead at the highest level was needed to build the three carriers envisaged by the programme, and the Soviet leaders had said no.

As the next-best solution, Marshal Dmitriy F. Ustinov (then with the CC of the Communist Party) proposed modifying Project 1123, as the *Moskva* class ASW carriers were designated. (**Note:** 'Defence Secretary' is **not** used in the meaning attached to this phrase in the US. Ustinov was not yet Minister of Defence then but, speaking in US terms, chairman of a standing committee handling defence matters.) Rather than upgrade the two existing Project 1123 ships, SNS *Moskva* and SNS *Leningrad*, a third carrier with increased displacement would be built; it would have a carrier wing comprising V/STOL fighters and helicopters. The next two carriers would be even more extensively modified, featuring steam catapults for launching MiG-23K and Su-25K CTOL fighters. (The designation Su-25K was reused for the export version of the single-seat Frogfoot; now the K suffix meant *kommehrcheskiy* ('commercial', ie, 'customer version'), not *korabel'nyy*.) The project was designated, somewhat enigmatically, 'large cruiser with aircraft armament', and the Ministry of Shipbuilding began finalising it with a view to commissioning two nuclear-powered carriers by 1985.

Since CTOL carriers were absolutely new to the Soviet Navy (the existing *Kiev*-class carriers had only Yakovlev Yak-36 *Forger* V/STOL strike aircraft), the deck catapult, arrestor wire installation and emergency barrier, optical and electronic landing aids and other things peculiar to carrier operation had to be perfected and mastered. To this end a special Research, Development and Training Complex (RDTC) was to be constructed at Novofyodorovka airbase near the city of Saki on the Crimea Peninsula, home to the AVMF Flight Test Centre. However, building the 'large cruisers' called for an upgrade of the existing shipyards; Gosplan (the Soviet Union's economic planning and budget management organisation) did not allocate extra

funds for this, and the 'large cruisers' were abandoned in favour of Project 1143 carriers. These would carry V/STOL aircraft, but the fifth Project 1143 carrier would be suitably modified for operating CTOL aircraft.

It should be noted here that the Soviet (Russian) carriers were, and still are, referred to as 'heavy aircraft-carrying cruisers'. The term was coined to find a way around an international treaty prohibiting the passage of aircraft carriers through the straits of Bosporus and Dardanelles. Since the carriers were built at the Black Sea shipyards, calling them by their proper name would mean they would be locked in the Black Sea, which of course was totally unacceptable.

As the Soviet aircraft carrier programme got under way the aircraft designers were immediately faced with the task of selecting the best take-off mode; they had to choose between a deck catapult and a ski jump. The catapult launch technique is certainly more common. The aircraft is hooked up to the catapult shoe, and as the catapult fires it accelerates to some 300 km/h (166 kts) as it clears the flight deck. Then it dips below deck level, pitching up to normal take-off angle of attack, and begins climbing normally. The high launch speed is required because the aircraft's angle of attack (AOA) on deck is close to zero and the launch trajectory is almost horizontal. Since the catapult track is only about 90 m (295 ft) long, the acceleration to 300 km/h is a violent experience; during launch the pilot is subjected to 4.5 Gs which often causes G-loc (G-induced loss of consciousness), impairing his ability to fly the aircraft.

Another peculiarity of catapult-launched aircraft is the necessity to increase the AOA (and thus lift) after disengagement from the catapult shoe in order to permit take-off with a full fuel and ordnance load. Therefore, catapult-launched aircraft are fitted with a so-called jump strut – a nose gear unit with an extra-extensible oleo which is extended forcibly to its full length. However, this requires the strut and forward fuselage to be reinforced, incurring a weight penalty and impairing performance.

The ill-starred T10K-1, the first prototype of the Su-27K, during a test flight. Note absence of the wing folding hinges.

Conversely, on a carrier equipped with a ski jump the aircraft is restrained by pop-up detents, allowing it to go to full afterburner before the detents are retracted. After leaving the ski jump the aircraft has a positive AOA and pitch angular speed; these increase as the aircraft accelerates, assisting climb. Thus, the pilot stays in control at all times, which enhances flight safety. The ski jump technique obviates the need for additional reinforcement of the nose gear and forward fuselage to absorb the extra loads generated by the catapult, saving weight and improving performance. On the other hand, the speed at which the aircraft clears the ski jump (120 to 140 km/h or 66 to 77 kts) is approximately twice lower than during catapult launch, which means especially stringent requirements apply to the aircraft's stability and controllability.

After carefully studying both options and analysing operational experience with shipboard fighters abroad, the Sukhoi and Mikoyan bureaux proposed that the future CTOL carrier should be equipped with a ski jump. This view was supported by LII, the Central Aerodynamics & Hydrodynamics Institute named after Nikolay Ye. Zhukovskiy

(TsAGI – *Tsen-**trahl**'nyy **aero**- i **ghid**rodi-na**mich**eskiy insti**toot***), the State Research Institute of Aircraft Systems (GosNII AS – *Gosoo**dahrst**vennyy na**oochno**-issle-dovatel'skiy insti**toot** aviatseeonnykh sistem*) and the MoD's Central Research Institute No. 30 (TsNII-30 – *Tsen-**trahl**'nyy na**oochno**-issledovatel'skiy insti**toot***).

In mid-1981 Marshal D. F. Ustinov, by then appointed Defence Minister, approved the proposal put forth by MAP and the VVS. This concerned ski jump take-off research with the MiG-29 and Su-27 fourth-generation fighters, which implied the new carrier would be equipped with a ski jump. However, the carrier wing was to consist mainly of Yakovlev Yak-41 (Yak-141) *Freestyle* supersonic V/STOL fighters, the MiG-29 and Su-27 being regarded as a 'second choice' in case the Yak-41 programme went wrong.

By mid-1982 the RDTC at Novofyodor-ovka AB in Saki was fully operational. The pompous and tongue-twisting official appellation NIUTK (*Na**oochno**-issledovatel'skiy i oo**cheb**no-treni**rov**ochnyy **kom**pleks – RDTC) soon gave way to the easily pronounceable nickname '*Nitka*' (Thread) which soon found its way into official documents as

well. (Shades of Ariadne's thread?) The complex comprised the T-1 ski jump (T = *tram**plin*** – ski jump), a rather provisional deck catapult and two arrestor systems – one with a cable, the other with a chain. The catapult, arrestor hook, S-2 arrestor wire installation and S-23N emergency barrier could be tested simultaneously. Ministry of Shipbuilding reps thoroughly tested them before flight tests commenced. A weighted trolley fitted with an arrestor hook was 'launched' by the catapult, catching the wire immediately afterwards; if the arrestor wire and the barrier failed, there was the chain arrestor as a last resort.

Carrier compatibility trials began next. Since the navalized Flanker and Fulcrum prototypes were not yet available, LII fitted a MiG-27 *Flogger-D* ground attack aircraft experimentally with an arrestor hook (the folding ventral fin had to be removed). This testbed was used to study the influence of the aircraft's weight and speed on arrestor wire engagement (both normal and offset) and the effect of G loads during deceleration on the pilot's system.

A section of a carrier's flight deck was built up at the 'Nitka' RDTC. This 'unsinkable carrier' was much used for carrier compatibility tests of new naval aircraft, verification of carrier equipment and pilot training.

Starting in 1983, the carrier (Project 1143.5) and the aircraft that were to operate from it were developed almost in parallel, the two ministries responsible for the programme (the Ministry of Shipbuilding and MAP) working in close co-operation. Yakovlev, Sukhoi and Mikoyan were all busy with naval fighter projects.

Trials performed on the Nitka complex in 1982-84 confirmed that the CTOL fighter/ski jump/arrestor wire combination was practicable. In 1984 the Communist Party Central Committee and the Council of Ministers issued a joint directive ordering the Mikoyan and Sukhoi bureaux to develop carrier-based versions of the MiG-29 and Su-27. It envisaged the T10-K (Su-27K) as a heavy shipboard interceptor and the MiG-29K as a lighter counter-air fighter with a secondary strike role. (It should be noted that initial studies in this direction dated back to 1973.)

True, the original plan for the MiG-29K to fill the air defence role for the carrier group, and it was with this fighter in mind that the carrier

was designed. Yet the Su-27, speaking figuratively, had a bunch of aces up its sleeve, namely longer range, high manoeuvrability, a more capable radar, ten hardpoints for assorted AAMs and, importantly, a high thrust-to-weight ratio and a low approach speed. All of this made it the prime contender for the Soviet Navy's shipboard fighter.

Sukhoi and Mikoyan began ski jump takeoff research in 1982 when the RDTC at Novofyodorovka AB became operational. Several development aircraft, including the third prototype Su-27 Flanker-A (T10-3, coded 310 Blue), were used for carrier operations research. Sukhoi OKB test pilot Nikolay F. Sadovnikov made the first take-offs from the T-1 ski jump in 1982.

The following year the T10-3 was retrofitted with an arrestor hook; so was the T10-25, an early-production Su-27 Flanker-B (25 Blue, c/n unknown, f/n 06-03) which featured a reinforced undercarriage into the bargain. The original T-1 ski jump turned out to be a lemon, and the two converted aircraft were used for extensive carrier landing trials while a reprofiled T-2 ski jump (which was much

closer to the real thing) was under construction. Between them, Nikolay F. Sadovnikov and LII test pilot Viktor G. Pugachov made more than 100 ski jump take-offs and arrestor wire engagements in 1982-84, proving that fourth-generation fighters could operate from an aircraft carrier without using a steam catapult. Later, NII VVS test pilots Col Yuriy A. Syomkin and Col V. M. Kandaoorov began operating from the 'unsinkable carrier'. However, the scope of the flight test programme was limited by the lack of further navalised aircraft.

Full-scale development of the shipboard Flanker known in-house as the T10-K began in 1984; the official designation Su-27K was assigned later. Mikhail P. Simonov supervised the programme but the actual design effort was led by chief project engineer Konstantin Marbashev. The aircraft was primarily intended for air defence (destruction of aircraft and helicopters, cruise missiles and UAVs); secondary roles included ground attack, anti-shipping strike and close air support (CAS).

Retaining the basic BWB layout of the Su-27, the T10-K introduced several features

Another view of the T10K-1 as it banks away from the camera ship. Unlike all subsequent Flanker-Ds, this aircraft lacked the wing and stabilator folding feature.

The T10K-1 during flight refuelling trials. The modified second prototype Su-27UB (T10U-2) equipped with an UPAZ-1A refuelling pod acts as the tanker.

associated with carrier operations. Firstly, small canard foreplanes were installed just aft of the cockpit (at the rear bulkhead of the forward fuselage), requiring the LERXes to be slightly reshaped. The arrangement had been tested on the T10-24 CCV mentioned in the introductory chapter; because of the canards the Russian press habitually called the T10-K a 'triplane', which it was not. The canards countered the pitch-down force generated by the LE and TE flaps, reducing approach speed 1.5 times, and acted as 'destabilizers' in supersonic cruise, reducing trim drag.

The vertical tails were shortened slightly, as the basic Su-27 was too tall to fit into the carrier's hangar. As befits a carrier-borne aircraft, the wings had power folding; unusually, so had the horizontal tail – a unique feature among shipboard fighters. Wing area was increased slightly but the span remained unchanged. The large flaperons of the land-based version gave way to two-section flaps, with small flaperons outboard of them replacing the Flanker-B's rigid trailing edge. The powerful TE flaps provided 50% more lift as compared to the land-based version,

markedly reducing approach speed. The LE flaps were lowered automatically.

The tail 'stinger' was shortened, reducing overall length. It accommodated the arrestor hook mechanism, hence the undersurface of the 'stinger' was flattened where the arrestor hook adhered to it. The brake parachute container normally housed in the tail 'stinger' was deleted, giving way to an L-006 (SPO-15) Beryoza (Birch) radar homing and warning system (RHAWS) enclosed by a dielectric fairing; hence the strakes housing RHAWS aerials on the engine nacelles of the land-based Flankers were also deleted. The tip of the tail 'stinger' and the nose radome folded upwards to save hangar space.

The navigation and communications suite included special equipment for overwater operations and carrier approach. The IRST 'ball' was offset to starboard to improve downward visibility during approach and landing. The wing folding mechanism caused a reduction in fuel capacity, so a retractable L-shaped refuelling probe offset to port was fitted immediately ahead of the windscreen to extend range.

The landing gear was beefed up to

absorb the increased load during no-flare landings characteristic of carrier operations. The single nosewheel and levered suspension of the basic Su-27 was replaced by two smaller wheels and an increased-stroke oleo; the mainwheels had heavy-duty increased-pressure tyres more resistant to wear and tear, permitting high gross weight take-offs. The mainwheel oleos incorporated tiedown shackles which were also used for hooking the aircraft to the aircraft handling conveyor belt in the hangar (called Mustang). Remarkably, the thicker oleos did not require larger main gear fairings.

The K-36DM ejection seat was set at 30° to help the pilot tolerate higher G loads. Finally, the whole airframe was reinforced to absorb the additional loads from the landing gear, canards and arrestor hook, and corrosion-resistant materials were used to protect the airframe and powerplant against the corrosive environment of the ocean.

The T10-K's systems and equipment were basically similar to those of the land-based Su-27, except for the actuators powering the canards, TE flaps, wing/stabilator folding mechanisms and arrestor hook. The

An evening shot of the T10K-2 on the deck of the aircraft carrier SNS *Tbilisi*.

avionics were also broadly similar. Like the standard land-based fighter, the T10-K had an N-001 Mech (RLPK-27) radar with a detection range of 80 to 100 km (44 to 55 nm) capable of tracking ten targets over land and sea and enabling the fighter to attack two targets at a time. The IRST had day and night passive tracking channels and was integrated with the NSTs-27 helmet-mounted sight (nashlemnaya sistema tseleookazahniya – HMS) assisting targeting in a dogfight when the pilot is subjected to high G forces.

The PNK-10K flight instrumentation and navigation suite (*pilotahzhno-navigatseeonnyy kompleks* [*dlya samolyota* T-]10) included an autopilot linked to an autothrottle. It enabled automatic route following with navigational inputs from LORAN and satellite navigation (GPS) systems, as well as automatic return to base and automatic carrier approach directed by the shipboard Resistor-K42 landing aid. The latter enabled ICAO Cat II automatic approach (horizontal visibility 400 m/1,312 ft, decision altitude 30 m/98 ft) and landing. The avionics working with the Resistor-K42 autoland system were put through their paces on the second prototype

Su-27UB (T10U-2) which thus became an avionics testbed. An active beacon was attached to the nose gear unit to provide a better radar signature. (The Su-27 is not a stealth aircraft, but the carrier's ATC radar is not very powerful either.)

The weapons control system and navigation suite could guide the aircraft to aerial targets automatically or using data downloaded by command link from a ship. Their features included automatic target search, lock-on and generation of missile launch commands. The aircraft turned away after firing the missiles (these were of the 'fire and forget' type) and repeated the sequence automatically if the need arose.

The T10-K featured data link equipment for co-ordinating group action, a multi-channel communications suite and comprehensive ECM gear; the latter included removable Sorbtsiya and L-203 Gardeniya (Gardenia) jammer pods in addition to built-in equipment. All avionics were virtually jam-proof, which was a must when operating in the intense electromagnetic environment aboard the carrier (the ship's own mission equipment generates a lot of interference).

Besides the built-in GSh-301 cannon and up to ten AAMs, the T10-K's armament included the 3M80 Moskit supersonic anti-shipping missile carried on the centreline on a special adapter. The naval Flanker had 12 hardpoints instead of ten; still, the ordnance load was limited to 6,500 kg (14,329 lb) – just 500 kg (1,102 lb) above that of the land-based version – because of the fighter's higher MTOW.

The aircraft would take off from one of the carrier's three take-off stations equipped with jet blast shields and pop-up mainwheel detents; the latter were retracted by an operator after the pilot selected full afterburner. Even using the station which afforded the shortest take-off run of only 105 m (344 ft), the Su-27K could take off easily with a full fuel and weapons load. The ski jump was inclined 15°; the normal glideslope angle during final approach was 4°.

Landing was possible in automatic, directed (command link) and manual mode. To this end the carrier was equipped with VOR/localizer and glideslope beacons, approach radar and a Luna-3 (Moon-3, pronounced loonah) visual approach slope indi-

The fourth prototype Su-27K (T10K-4, 59 Blue) on a hardstand at LII, Zhukovskiy.

Test pilot Viktor Pugachov climbs into the cockpit of the sixth naval prototype (T10K-6).

cator (VASI). The fighter approached the carrier in a steep descent, touching down without flaring out, and the arrestor hook caught one of the arrestor wires raised 10 to 15 cm (4 to 6 in.) above the deck, bringing the aircraft to a standstill. If the arrestor hook missed the wires the pilot could apply full throttle and make a go-around. An emergency barrier could be erected if a damaged

aircraft was coming in or if the pilot was wounded.

The advanced development project of the T10-K shipboard fighter was approved by the Powers That Be in 1984, and prototype construction got under way. Coded 37 Blue, the first prototype (T10K-1) was completed in the spring of 1987 and made its first flight on 17th August at the hands of Viktor G. Pugachov. This aircraft retained the wings and horizontal tail of the basic Su-27 because the wing and stabilator folding mechanisms were not flight-cleared at the time. The second prototype designated T10K-2 (39 Blue) joined the flight test programme almost exactly a year later; it incorporated wing/stabilator folding and all other features included in the project.

Both aircraft underwent large-scale testing at Novofyodorovka AB where Sukhoi and NII VVS test pilots perfected ski jump take-off and carrier landing techniques. The airframe changes, systems and avionics were verified during a lengthy test programme, with G. G. Smotritskiy as engineer in charge. Unfortunately, the trials did not go altogether without mishap. The first prototype was lost when it failed to recover from a flat spin; Nikolay F. Sadovnikov was injured during ejection, which put an end to his flying career. Pugachov became project test pilot and bore the brunt of the trials programme, flying the T10K-2 and the T10-25 (the latter served as a substitute until more prototypes became available).

The manufacturer's flight test programme was completed within a short time frame because many of the T10-K's features had already been verified on various testbeds. However, the carrier compatibility issue remained unresolved because the carrier was still under construction at the Black Sea Shipyard in Nikolayev (the Ukraine). Laid down pursuant to order No. 0-105 as SNS *Riga* on 1st April 1982 (some April Fool's Day joke, indeed), the ship was renamed SNS *Leonid Brezhnev* in November 1982 and launched on 6th December 1985. In August 1987 the still-unfinished carrier was rechristened again, becoming SNS *Tbilisi*, and it was under this name that she was commissioned. (Speaking of which, the Soviet Navy seemed to have a tradition of naming its aircraft carriers after Soviet cities. In addition to the Project 1123 helicopter carriers SNS *Moskva* and SNS *Loningrad*, the four 'true' V/STOL aircraft carriers were named SNS *Kiev*, SNS *Minsk*, SNS *Novorossiysk* and SNS *Baku*.)

Carrier compatibility trials were scheduled to begin in the autumn of 1989, even though SNS *Tbilisi* was not 100% complete by then. They would show if the carrier met the aircraft designers' requirements and if the Navy's fighter pilot training techniques were correct. On 21st October 1989 the carrier put to sea for the first time pursuant to a joint directive of MAP, the Ministry of Shipbuilding, the VVS and the Navy, sailing from Nikolayev

The T10K-6 (in the foreground) and the T10K-5 on the ramp in Zhukovskiy. Note that the T10K-5 is equipped with Sorbtsiya ECM pods.

Shipboard fighters parked like this (in 'carrier fashion' to save deck space) are an unusual sight at an ordinary airfield.

The T10K-6 in the demonstration hangar at the New Equipment Demonstration Centre, Kubinka AB.

to the Navy base at Sevastopol' for official delivery to the Navy.

Seagoing trials commenced at the end of the month. Before a landing could be risked, Sukhoi and NII VVS pilots trained day after day, mastering the unfamiliar no-flare landing technique. The second prototype Su-27K (T10K-2) and ordinary Flanker-Bs made low passes over the carrier; the T10K-2's first overflight was on 27th October. On his final try that day Viktor Pugachov passed just 30 m (98 ft) over the deck with an ear-splitting roar, forcing everyone on deck to plug their ears and drop to a crouch. The men working on the ski jump were worse off than the rest, since the structure rises nearly 7 m (23 ft) above the flight deck. Each pilot was to make some 400 landings on the 'unsinkable carrier' in Saki before he was cleared for real-life carrier landings.

Initially the flights progressed with *Tbilisi* standing at anchor with her bows to the wind; later flights were made while the carrier moved at 10... 13 kts on various headings. Overflights at progressively lower altitude were soon followed by touch-and-gos. On 31st October the State commission accepting the carrier held a meeting aboard the *Tbilisi*, clearing the carrier for her first 'real' landing.

On 1st November 1989 the T10K-2 flown by Viktor G. Pugachov successfully made the first conventional carrier landing in Soviet history. At 1:46 PM local time the fighter touched down, catching the second wire, and came to a halt after a landing run of about 90 m (295 ft). The aircraft rolled back a little, disengaging itself from the wire, then Pugachov raised the arrestor hook, folded the wings and taxied up to the island. As the engines died down and the canopy opened, deck hands were already running towards the aircraft with a portable ladder, followed by the beaming officials.

More thrills (and spills) came next day when the first take-off was attempted. When

Viktor Pugachov concluded his spectacular flying display in the Su-27K at the MAKS-97 airshow with a 'waltz' in the middle of the runway as the aircraft folded the wings and stabilators.

Overall view of the T10K-6 in 'parking configuration' with the wings and stabilators folded.

A view of the T10K-6's wing folding joint.

Above: The T10K-5 with Sorbtsiya ECM pods.

Left: The T10K-4 on a snow-covered hardstand during trials.

Below: The T10K-6 lines up for take-off. Note the phototheodolite calibration markings.

As this view shows, the T10K-5 carried the tactical code on the port side only.

Above: The T10K-6 taxies in after completing its demo flight at MAKS-97.

Top and above: Viktor Pugachov demonstrates a carrier approach with the arrestor hook down.

A production Su-27K (Su-33) makes a dawn take-off from the T-2 ski jump at Novofyodorovka AB, Saki.

A Russian Navy (279th Shipboard Fighter Regiment/1st Sqn) Su-33 makes a practice landing on the Nitka carrier training complex in Saki.

A rare shot of a pair of Su-27Ks (Su-33s) in formation flight.

the wheel detents and blast shield were raised into position Simonov claimed that, at the nominal deflection of 60°, the shield was too close to the fighter's engine nozzles. He ordered it set at 45°, but the actuator could not hold the shield in that position. To cure the problem, makeshift braces made of steel pipes were welded to the deck to hold the shield at the required angle.

The T10K-2 was towed to take-off station 1 on the starboard side ahead of the island. When Pugachov engaged the afterburners, the wheel detents would not retract. As a result, the aircraft sat in front of the blast shield for 14 seconds instead of six seconds, the engines running in full afterburner all the time; the shield's water cooling system overheated and blew up spectacularly. Six cooling system modules were torn out and savagely twisted, and the thing could only be repaired at the shipyard. Still, the aircraft suffered no damage, so it was towed to a spot on the port take-off line halfway between stations 2 and 3. From there Pugachov took off without using detents or blast shields. After a steep climb the fighter circled, performed the famous Cobra manoeuvre and departed for Saki.

Thus ended Stage 1 of the trials programme. The T10K's flights were suspended while test equipment records were analysed and assorted problems rectified. In the meantime, NII VVS pilots Yuriy A. Syomkin and S. S. Rossoshanskiy each made several passes over the carrier on standard Su-27s.

The flights resumed on 10th November. On 21st November Pugachov made the first night landing in the T10K-2, and the carrier compatibility trials were successfully com-

pleted the following day. Between them the participating aircraft – the T10K-2, the first prototype MiG-29K (311 Blue) and the prototype Su-25UTG (08 Blue) – had made 227 flights in 24 shifts. Of the 35 arrestor wire engagements made by the three aircraft, 13 were made by Pugachov in the T10K-2.

In late 1989, even before the MiG-29K and Su-27K had completed their respective flight test programmes, the latter aircraft was cleared for full-scale production in Komsomol'sk-on-Amur. In the meantime, pre-production Su-27Ks were already on the KnAAPO assembly line. The third prototype, designated T10K-3 (c/n unknown, f/n 02-01), had no tactical code, though logically it should have been 49 Blue. The aircraft made its maiden flight on 17th February 1990. (The Su-27K has a separate fuselage number sequence. Batch 1 consisted of a single airframe (f/n 01-01) used for static tests.)

The fourth prototype, T10K-4 (59 Blue, c/n 49051002502, f/n 02-02), had the tactical code applied in smaller digits than the other aircraft. On 18th August 1991, it made the type's public debut at the Aviation Day flypast in Zhukovskiy.

The fifth development aircraft, T10K-5 (69 Blue, c/n 49051002603, f/n 02-02), wore a non-standard overall grey colour scheme rather than the usual deep blue of naval Flankers. On 11th-16th August 1992 it was in the static display at MosAeroShow '92 in Zhukovskiy, carrying a 3M80 Moskit anti-shipping missile marked ASM-MSS ('air-to-surface missile/missile supersonique'; this is the export designation) on the centreline station. The sixth aircraft (T10K-6, 79 Blue;

c/n unknown, f/n 03-01) was demonstrated to top-ranking Soviet government and military officials at Machoolischchi AB on 13th February 1992. Two months later, on 11th April, the same aircraft armed with a Moskit ASM was in the static park at the Kubinka-92 open doors day.

These aircraft were followed by the T10K-7 (probably 89 Blue, c/n unknown, f/n 03-02), the uncoded T10K-8 (should have been 99 Blue; c/n unknown, f/n 03-03) and the final prototype, T10K-9 (109 Blue, c/n 49051003604, f/n 03-04). Originally wearing the tactical code on the port side only, the latter aircraft was displayed at the MAKS-95 (22nd-27th August 1995), Ghelendzhik-96 (September 1996) and MAKS-97 (19th-24th August 1997) airshows, both on the ground and in flight. At MAKS-97 the T10K-9 carried a full weapons load: a Moskit ASM, four R-60M 'dogfight missiles', four R-27ER radar-homing AAMs and two R-27ET IR-homing AAMs. The rudders were painted in Russian flag colours and the port air intake was adorned by a badge reading '*Za dahl'niy pokhod*' ([awarded] for a long-range cruise – ie, the carrier's Mediterranean cruise of 1995-96), three anchors and the figures 105 marking the number of carrier landings to date.

There was a good deal of flying in the summer of 1990 when SNS *Tbilisi* was going through her manufacturer's trials and State acceptance trials. The Navy and the designers tried to get the ship and the aircraft functioning perfectly in tune. Still, the flight test programme was not completed, despite the fact that three Su-27Ks (the second, third and fourth prototypes) were operating from the *Tbilisi* along with other aircraft. No concerted action training or live weapons trials were held, and the intercept missions in concert with an A-50 AWACS aircraft were rather too brief because time was running short.

(The 'other aircraft' operating from the carrier were both MiG-29K prototypes (311 Blue and 312 Blue), a Su-25UTG, Kamov Ka-27PS Helix-C SAR helicopters, Ka-29 Helix-B assault choppers and the second prototype Ka-31 AEW helicopter (032 Blue). Curiously, the latter sported the Soviet flag and *Ghidromettsentr* titles, masquerading as a civil weather research aircraft!)

On October 4, 1990 the carrier was rechristened once again, becoming SNS *Admiral Kuznetsov*. (The full official name is SNS *Admirahl Flota Sovetskovo Soyooza Nikolay Kuznetsov* – Flt Adm Nikolay Kuznetsov.) The final stage of her State acceptance trials scheduled for the summer of 1991 was to include 110 flights and aerodynamic testing of the jet blast shields which were still a major source of problems. Sukhoi test pilots Sergey N. Mel'nikov and Vyacheslav Yu. Aver'yanov and Mikoyan test pilot Roman P. Taskayev did a lot of flying at this stage (Taskayev had superseded Aubakirov who had begun training for a space mission). However, the political situation in the USSR was rapidly turning into untold chaos. Shortages of jet fuel and fuel oil for the carrier and, more importantly, the necessity to urgently prepare the ship for transition to the Northern Fleet forced a premature termination of the trials. The flights were suspended and SNS *Admiral Kuznetsov* was firmly anchored at the Navy base in Novorossiysk.

In the first days of December 1991 the carrier sailed from Novorossiysk, commanded by Capt. (1st grade) V. S. Yarygin. She was on her way to a new port of registry, taking with her fifteen pilots and more than forty technicians of the 100th KIAP (*korabel'nyy istrebitel'nyy aviapolk* – shipboard fighter regiment). The unit was formed at Novofyodorovka AB on 10th March 1986 specially for training the fifth Soviet carrier's fighter pilots; its CO, Col Timur A. Apakidze, was the first service pilot to make a 'real' CTOL carrier landing. With Russia and the Ukraine quarrelling over the Black Sea Fleet, the political climate in Novorossiysk was rapidly becoming too cold for comfort, and it was decided to move the carrier before the Ukraine could lay a claim on her.

In 1992 the carrier put to sea again – this time as RNS (Russian Navy ship) *Admiral Kuznetsov*, since the Soviet Union was dead and buried by then. The objective this time was to hold State acceptance trials of the Su-27K; the fighter passed them with flying colours and was included into the AVMF inventory in October 1994. The naval version received the ASCC code name Flanker-D.

As mentioned earlier, the Su-27K entered production in Komsomol'sk-on-Amur in 1992. Later the aircraft received the unofficial designation Su-33, and Sukhoi obstinately refer to it as such.

The political turmoil that swept the former Soviet Union led to further delays in the carrier's trials and service entry. It was not until the autumn of 1992 that RNS *Admiral Kuznetsov* sailed into the Barents Sea to perform flight tests of production Su-27Ks equipping her carrier wing and conduct pilot training on Su-25UTGs. Sukhoi test pilot Sergey Mel'nikov was obliged to do both tasks, since Viktor Pugachov was busy with the Su-27M (Su-35) programme and there were no other pilots qualified to act as instructors.

Saki and hence the Nitka training complex was in the newly-independent Ukraine which was at odds with Russia over the Black Sea Fleet issue. This meant that 'live' flying from the carrier was the only way of training naval pilots. However, this was obviously impractical because of the increased wear on the carrier, so the Russian military had to start negotiations in order to regain access to the base in Saki. Eventually it was decided

In the summer of 1999 and 2000, 279th KIAP pilots visited Saki to take proficiency training.

A Su-33 comes in for a 'carrier landing'.

Regular training at Novofyodorovka AB enables 279th KIAP pilots to stay current, maintaining their carrier operations skills.

An evening scene at Novofyodorovka AB, Saki.

that Russia would rent the complex; an inter-governmental agreement was signed and the complex, which had been put in storage, was reactivated.

By then aircraft factory No. 99 in Ulan-Ude had completed a small batch of produc-tion Su-25UTG trainers. In mid-1994 the first ten pilots of the 279th KIAP (formerly 100th KIAP) began flying Su-27Ks and Su-25UTGs from the 'unsinkable carrier'. In July and August the unit's pilots made 167 arrestor wire engagements and 69 ski jump take-offs. Such intensive training was unheard of even in Soviet times, but it was this that enabled all of the unit's pilots to get their carrier opera-tions rating within a very short time frame.

By the end of August all 24 production Su-27Ks (Su-33s) had joined the *Admiral Kuznetsov* in Severomorsk, a Russian Navy and naval aviation base which was the carri-er's port of registry. On 31st August 1994 Igor' S. Kozhin became the first of the origi-nal ten pilots trained at Novofyodorovka to make a carrier landing, followed soon after by V. V. Doobovoy and Konstantin B. Kochkaryov. In the few days that followed, G. B. Ryzhov, Pavel E. Podgoozov, Andrey A. Abramov and other pilots landed on the car-rier. After making a few more landings each in order to get accustomed, the pilots began flying intercept sorties over the Barents Sea.

On 9th May 1995, five 279th KIAP Su-27Ks participated in the grand military parade on Poklonnaya Gora in Moscow to mark the 50th anniversary of VE-Day. The formation was led by Col Timur A. Apakidze,

by then promoted to CO of the 57th SKAD (*smeshannaya korabel'naya aviadiveeziya* – composite shipboard air division; later he rose in rank to Major General). Three weeks earlier eight of the unit's aircraft had arrived at Kubinka AB to train for the parade because naval fighter pilots have little formation flying experience.

In the summer of 1995 six Su-27Ks and two Su-25UTGs were 'deployed' to Novofyodorovka AB where the first ten pilots took proficiency training and a fresh group of pilots took the whole carrier operations course. In eleven flight shifts the pilots made a total of 398 flights involving 797 touch-downs (including 125 wire engagements) and 74 ski jump take-offs, receiving or con-firming their carrier ratings.

Meanwhile the carrier had been over-hauled at the shipyard in Murmansk, and in October she took part in a large-scale Northern Fleet exercise. This was a sort of final test before the *Admiral Kuznetsov*'s first long-range cruise which began on 23rd December 1995.

Chronologically the cruise went as follows. On 7th December the carrier put to sea; two days later Sergey Mel'nikov flew the ninth prototype Su-27K (109 Blue) from Zhukovskiy to Severomorsk-3 AB. On 11th December pilots Kritskiy and Bogdan made practice flights in two production aircraft at the same location. Next day four Su-27Ks landed on the carrier; two were ferried by 929th GLITs test pilot Diorditsa, the other two by test pilots Rayevskiy (929th GLITs) and

Mel'nikov (Sukhoi OKB). 279th KIAP pilots made three more flights before the end of the year (one on 21st December and two on 29th December).

279th KIAP operations during the cruise went as follows. Three flights were made on 4th January 1996, five more next day. Then came a pause until 19th January when eight flights were made; ten flights followed on 20th January, 20 flights on 21st January, eleven on 22nd January, eighteen on 23rd January, 21 on 26th January and twelve on 27th January.

On 3rd February the *Admiral Kuznetsov* had to drop anchor because the engines broke down. Two flights were made on 5th February, 21 flights next day, nineteen on 7th February, thirteen on 12th February, 21 on 14th February and seven on 16th February. 15th February was wasted because the car-rier's engines broke down again, and on 19th-20th February the ship could move only at half speed ahead to avoid further damage to the powerplant.

Normal operations did not resume until 1st March, but that was the biggest flying day, with 25 flights. Ten flights followed on 2nd March, fourteen on 3rd March, twelve on 17th March, six on 18th March, three on 20th March and nine more next day.

The cruise ended on 25th March 1996. Within this time frame the carrier had entered the Mediterranean via the Atlantic Ocean, visiting Malta and Syria when the training objectives were completed. A Russian naval delegation paid a visit to the carrier USS *America*; the Americans even went so far as to give Maj Gen Apakidze a ride in a Grumman A-6 Intruder strike aircraft. Not to be outdone, Russian naval pilots amazed the Americans with their flying skill when two Su-27Ks streaked between RNS *Admiral Kuznetsov* and the missile frigate USS *Monterey* almost at zero level. (The *Monterey* had put in an appearance a few days earlier and had been shadowing RNS *Admiral Kuznetsov* since then.) Apakidze also made his mark, giving an impressive aerobatics display.

This unprecedentedly long cruise for a Russian carrier gave the pilots a taste of fly-ing in various climatic and geographic zones; practice patrol flights were made in the immediate vicinity of US Navy 6th Fleet carri-er groups. The importance of the cruise was patently obvious, even though the *Admiral Kuznetsov* carried only seven production air-craft and one prototype. Maj. Gen. Apakidze and Col. Ivan I. Bokhonko, the 279th KIAP's new CO, received the Hero of Russia title for the cruise.

However, the cruise revealed numerous shortcomings of the ship and her aircraft. Among other things, the carrier's AD radar was inoperative because it was designed in the Ukraine and part of the radar set had not been installed due to the break-up of the USSR. This, and the fact that the Su-27K's radar and ESM suite were not working as they should, rendered the fighters 'blind' to enemy action; they were not only incapable of organising an effective air defence of the carrier group but open to attack. On one occasion a Su-27K was jumped by Israeli Defence Force/Air Force fighters off the Syrian coast. The Israeli jets began hemming the Russian fighter in, apparently attempting to force it down on Israeli territory, and the pilot had to make sharp manoeuvres in order to escape. The Flanker's ESM system did not give any warning, and the pilot did not realise he had company until it was almost too late.

When the carrier returned to Severomorsk, flight operations in the 279th KIAP wound down sharply. The fighters were grounded by fuel shortages and malfunctions most of the time; one particular problem area was unavailability of new tyres because their production had been suspended due to lack of funding. One of the few spells of activity came in the summer of 1996 when four of the unit's aircraft participated in a flypast over the Neva River in St. Petersburg during the Russian Navy's 300th anniversary celebration. The mission was to escort a Tu-142MZ *Bear F Mod* ASW aircraft, the flagship of Russia's naval air arm, so five Su-27Ks were detached to Ostrov AB near Pskov (the AVMF training centre) where the *Bear* was based.

The various problems keeping the Su-27Ks on the ground were beginning to affect flight safety, as the pilots were getting 'rusty'. While practising for the anniversary flypast, Andrey A. Abramov misjudged a manoeuvre and collided with another fighter, slightly damaging it (luckily, both aircraft landed safely). The cause was plainly pilot error and Abramov should have been grounded, but the underlying reason was that the experienced pilot had not flown for a long time; grounding him would only make it worse. Besides, when a pilot has an accident through no fault of his own it is important to send him on another mission again as soon as possible before he loses his nerve. Understanding this, division CO Maj Gen Apakidze did everything to defend the pilot – one of his best pilots – in front of the air accident investigation board.

On 18th August 1996 several naval aircraft, including a Tu-142MZ escorted by four Su-27Ks, took part in the Aviation Day flypast at Moscow-Tushino. The leftmost fighter in the formation was flown by 57th SKAD deputy CO Col Vlasov. A month later he died in Saki during a proficiency training session...

In late 1996, 279th KIAP pilots trained at Novofyodorovka AB on Su-25UTGs; however, the *Admiral Kuznetsov*'s next cruise planned for the end of the year had to be cancelled because the carrier was still undergo-

In a few seconds this Su-27K (Su-33) will catch the wire. Note the T10M-9 on the carrier's deck.

279th KIAP pilots practise refuelling techniques.

ing repairs in Murmansk. By November the job was only 20% completed because of funding shortages.

In May 1997 three 279th KIAP pilots, including Timur A. Apakidze, went to Zhukovskiy to practice flight refuelling techniques at LII. In the summer of 1997 the unit participated in a Northern Fleet exercise, flying top cover for Red Force ships and intercepting Blue Force aircraft in a remote area of the Barents Sea. (In Soviet/Russian military exercises, Red Force is the 'good guys' and Blue Force is the 'bad guys'; in the West it is vice versa.) The group of twelve Flankers led by Maj Gen Apakidze destroyed several targets with R-60M (AA-8 *Aphid*) IR-homing 'dogfight missiles'. This was the first time the Su-27K fired short-range AAMs; even test pilots had not done it before.

Tactics were devised long before the exercise and the pilots did a good deal of training. The unit's weaponry engineers Capt Sergey Koorsekov and Capt Sergey Doobodelov had a hard time integrating the missiles with the aircraft because the Su-27K's weapons control system still had a lot of bugs (there had been no time to eliminate them before the type entered production). Nevertheless, the weaponry engineers accomplished their job in a remarkably short time, using special test equipment.

The Su-27K's show of force at the exercise was all the more impressive in view of the current plight of Russia's military aviation. In 1997 alone, the fuel and spares allowances approved at the beginning of the year were slashed twice – first by 30%, then by another 20%. Sixteen of the unit's aircraft had engine problems which could not be fixed *in situ*, requiring the engines to be shipped to overhaul plants. Still, all preparations for the exercise were completed in time.

Other complications arose during the exercise; the designated area which the fighters were to patrol was unexpectedly changed shortly before take-off. The professionalism of navigator-programmers Lt Col Vladimir Stetsenko and Lt Col Konstantin Kochkaryov saved the day; they quickly reprogrammed the fighters' navigation computers to suit the change in tactics.

Flanker pilots participating in the exercise included division CO Maj Gen Timur Apakidze, regiment CO Col Ivan Bokhonko, Col Pavel Kretov, Lt Col Pavel Podgoozov, Lt Col Andrey Abramov, Lt Col Sergey Rasskazov, Lt Col Valeriy Khvezhenko and five other top-class pilots. Having received a report of 'enemy aircraft' approaching Severomorsk-3 AB, the twelve pilots took off to repel the 'attack'.

Six aircraft then returned to base, while the other six proceeded to the missile range. Flare bombs dropped by other aircraft served as targets for the heat-seeking missiles, since the bombs have a high IR signature. Of course, they are a poor substitute for an aircraft making evasive manoeuvres, but still they descend fast and are hard to hit. Nevertheless, all six pilots scored 'kills' with their first missile. At the debriefing the pilots' marksmanship earned praise from the Northern Fleet Air Arm's combat training chief, Sniper Pilot (an official grade reflecting pilot expertise) Igor' Kozhin. A week later six other pilots successfully destroyed their targets with 'dogfight missiles' in adverse weather. The exercise included a number of night sorties. On the whole the pilots did not spend a lot of time in the air; still, they had the chance to master new combat tactics.

More proficiency training at Novofyodorovka AB came in August-September 1997 and August-September 1999 as 279th KIAP pilots trained for the *Admiral Kuznetsov*'s planned ocean cruises, using Su-27Ks (Su-33s) and Su-25UTGs. Besides the usual ski-jump take-offs and carrier landings, Su-27K pilots practised refuelling from a sister aircraft fitted with an UPAZ-1A 'buddy' refuelling pack ('Flanker tanker'); IFR training took place both in Saki and in Zhukovskiy.

October 1999 marked another 'first' in Russian naval aviation history – a Su-27K made the first night-time carrier landing beyond the Polar circle in adverse weather. The event was unique in that the landings were performed by ordinary service pilots (albeit very experienced ones) in the adverse weather conditions of the polar region; test pilots were not involved. Maj Gen Timur Apakidze (Hero of Russia), Col Igor' Kozhin (Hero of Russia) and Col Pavel Kretov got the

distinction of making these landings.

The carrier's next Mediterranean cruise was scheduled for the autumn of 2000; hence 279th KIAP pilots and technicians went through a period of intensive training at Novofyodorovka between July and mid-August. The training session was supervised by unit CO Igor' Kozhin and Timur Apakidze, who was appointed Deputy C-in-C of the Russian naval air arm by then.

In August 2000 RNS *Admiral Kuznetsov* put to sea as planned, heading for the North Fleet's training area in the Barents Sea. Her crew was tasked with supporting the operations of the carrier's air wing and checking the ship's manoeuvrability at different speeds. It was also planned to refresh the pilots' overwater operations skills, check the interaction between the carrier and other ships in the carrier group, and verify the group's joint air defence. Still, the cruise was cancelled because of the tragic loss of the nuclear-powered missile submarine RNS *Kursk* (K-141) in the Barents Sea on 12th August. A massive search and rescue effort was mounted (sadly, to no avail), and the Russian MoD diverted the funds originally allocated for the cruise to this operation.

The need for a dedicated trainer version of the Su-27K (Su-33) grew increasingly acute, since the subsonic Su-25UTG was no match for the Flanker-D in terms of performance. Hence the Sukhoi OKB started work on the T10KM-2 project (*kora**bel**'nyy, modifit-* ***see***rovannyy, dvookh***mest***nyy – shipboard, modified, two-seat). Far from being a straightforward adaptation of the land-based Su-27UB Flanker-C (T10-U), the naval trainer had a totally redesigned and much wider forward fuselage with side-by-side seating for the trainee and instructor. This facilitated crew communication and afforded both crew members an excellent downward field of view – an all-important feature for a carrier-based aircraft.

However, the defence budget cuts of the late 1980s which hampered the Soviet aircraft carrier programme inevitably took their toll on carrier-borne aircraft development. The Navy's interest in the trainer waned and the project was shelved. Still, Sukhoi engineers persisted with the side-by-side seating idea, hoping it would turn the Su-27 into a whole family of special mission aircraft – a shipboard strike aircraft, a tactical reconnaissance aircraft, an aerial refuelling tanker and even an AWACS platform (!). Eventually the idea materialised as the T10-V tactical bomber described in Chapter 3.

Operational experience showed that the Su-25UTG was not fully adequate for training Su-27K pilots in take-off and landing techniques. This led Sukhoi to dust off the idea of a dedicated naval trainer based on the T10-K. The new project bore the designation

T10-KU (*korabel'nyy, oochebnyy* [*samolyot*] – shipboard trainer). A full-scale mock-up of the forward fuselage was built by KnAAPO and inspected by the Navy, including 279th KIAP personnel.

Funding shortages caused the project to be put on hold, as the Russian MoD was unable to finance development of new military hardware. Fortunately, this situation did not last long. As already mentioned, the *Admiral Kuznetsov*'s first long-range cruise to the Mediterranean in 1995-96 highlighted the strengths and weaknesses of the ship and the Su-27K (Su-33). Flanker-D pilots were growing increasingly vocal about the lack of a trainer version. Thus the T10-KU project was reactivated in 1996, incorporating changes based on Mediterranean cruise experience. More importantly, the ideology of the project changed; the new aircraft was to be a multirole fighter rather than just a trainer.

The aircraft could best be described as the T10KM-2 project revisited, incorporating major structural and, first of all, aerodynamic changes. These concerned mainly the wings: wing span is increased from 14.7 m (48 ft 2.74 in.) to 16.0 m (52 ft 5.92 in.) and wing area from 62 m² (666.66 sq. ft) to 70 m² (752.68 sq. ft). The T10-KU was the first Russian combat aircraft to feature direct lift control: the high-lift devices adapted automatically to the prevailing flight conditions. This provided optimum lift in cruise mode and during manoeuvres, improving agility and increasing range. A special elastic seal closed the gap between the LE flaps and the wings, ensuring smooth airflow when the flaps were down.

The wing folding joints were moved outboard approximately 1.5 m (4 ft 11 in.) on each side so that the inner wing span matched the horizontal tail span; thus the T10-KU required slightly more space for deck/hangar storage as compared to the Su-27K. The wing folding angles were reduced, the outer wings being almost vertical when folded. The new wings were designed by Su-27K project chief Konstantin Marbashev.

The canards were enlarged and re-shaped (their tips were no longer parallel to the fuselage axis; this measure was meant to aid stealth). Horizontal tail area and rudder area were also increased; unlike the production Su-27K, the aircraft did not have the stabilator folding feature.

The forward fuselage was heavily modified. The T10-KU had a Su-34-style cockpit with side-by-side seating accessed from below via the nosewheel well. Apart from the reasons mentioned previously (crew communication and visibility), this arrangement was chosen because in an aircraft with stepped-tandem seating the back-seater would find it hard to use the VASI. This is important, since an aircraft carrier's VASI imposes strict limits

The Su-27KUB did not take part in the demonstration flights at the MAKS-99 airshow. On 21st August, however, the spectators had a chance to see it fly.

With the landing gear just beginning to retract, the Su-27KUB climbs out on a test flight from Zhukovskiy on 21st August 1999.

on the pilot's eye level during final approach. In the T10-KU, both crew members enjoyed almost identical conditions.

But here the similarity ended. The T10-KU had a conventional ogival radome instead of the Su-34's characteristic flattened nose. This was dictated by the type of radar installed on the naval two-seater. Originally the aircraft was to be equipped with a proven NIIP N-011 phased-array radar. Like the other aircraft of the 'Su-30 series', the aircraft had a fully-retractable L-shaped IFR probe on the port side; in stowed position this protruded a little more than on the abovementioned types.

The 'hump' aft of the cockpit was not as pronounced as on the Su-34. Also, an IRST 'ball' (absent on the bomber version) was installed ahead of the windscreen; unlike the Su-27K, it was located on the centreline, not offset to starboard. The production T10-KU will make use of LLLTV and thermal imaging equipment, as well as a self-contained precision navigation system.

The rest of the airframe is pretty much the same as on the Su-27K, including the heavy-duty landing gear optimised for no-flare landings, with twin 620x180 mm (24.4x7.08 in.) nosewheels and single 1,030x350 mm (40.55x13.77 in.) mainwheels. The nose unit retracts forward, not aft as on the Su-34; hence the cockpit access ladder is located ahead of the nose gear, not aft, and is almost vertical when lowered. Of course, the nosewheel well had to be widened somewhat as compared with the fighter in order to accom-

modate the ladder and ensure comfortable passage for the crew. No changes were made to the tail 'stinger', engine nacelles and fins. The number of weapons hardpoints and the internal cannon in the starboard LERX remained unchanged as well.

Overall length was identical to that of the Su-27K. So was gross weight – the Navy insisted on this. Sukhoi engineers managed to avoid a weight increase by making large-scale use of composites.

Given the scarcity of state funding, the Sukhoi OKB and KnAAPO had to provide much of the money needed to accelerate T10-KU development. At this stage the aircraft received the official designation Su-27KUB (*korabel'nyy, oochebno-boyevoy* [*samolyot*] – shipboard combat trainer); the aircraft is

The Su-27KUB taxies in after completing a test flight.

Close-up of the Su-27KUB's cockpit. Note the refuelling probe and the centralliy located IRST 'ball'.

sometimes referred to as the Su-33UB – or even Su-33KUB, which does not make sense.

The second pre-production Su-27K (T10K-4, 59 Blue) was set aside for conversion as the Su-27KUB prototype. In the second half of 1998 the fighter was 'chopped up' at Sukhoi's experimental shop in Moscow and mated with a new forward fuselage and other components delivered by KnAAPO. The new airframe subassemblies were painted in various shades of primer – the forward fuselage was chrome yellow, the folding outer wing panels were bright green etc.; this, together with the original (and well-weathered) blue camouflage on the rest of the airframe, gave the aircraft a distinctive patchwork appearance. (In fact, the dielectric portions of the fins, which were medium grey originally, had different colours at a later stage – white to port and green to starboard, obviously borrowed from two different aircraft!)

Wearing no tactical code, the prototype was rolled out in the spring of 1999. On 29th April 1999 the Su-27KUB successfully made its first flight in Zhukovskiy with pilot Viktor G. Pugachov and WSO Sergey Mel'nikov at the controls. Both crew members had the Hero of Russia title, specialised in the Sukhoi OKB's naval programmes and had participated in the first Mediterranean cruise of RNS *Admiral Kuznetsov* along with service pilots. The maiden flight lasted 30 minutes. Russian Navy C-in-C Adm Vladimir Kooroyedov, Naval Air Arm Commander Col Gen Vladimir G. Deyneka and former Maj Gen Timur A. Apakidze were there to witness the event.

By early June the aircraft had made seven test flights; young Sukhoi test pilot Roman Kondrat'yev took part in the tests together with Pugachov and Mel'nikov. The official rollout for the press was originally planned for mid-summer but then postponed until the MAKS-99 airshow (17th-22nd August 1999). Officially the *koobik* (little cube), as the aircraft was inevitably dubbed, was a no-show. Yet you have to know the Sukhoi people; one might be justified in saying that 'Su' stands for 'Surprise'. On Saturday, 21st August (which was the busiest day of the flying display programme), the still-unpainted and unmarked Su-27KUB suddenly appeared on the runway. After waiting at the holding position (and showing off for the crowds) for a few minutes it took off and was gone. About an hour later the aircraft came back and landed, elegantly displaying its other side. Those who decided to skip Saturday's flights sure missed a lot!

Manufacturer's flight tests continued until mid-summer 2000. Among other things, in late summer 1999 the Su-27KUB paid a visit to Novofyodorovka AB, Saki, to make its first ski-jump take-offs and carrier landings on the Nitka RDTC. In the autumn of 1999 the aircraft commenced carrier compatibility trials aboard the *Admiral Kuznetsov*.

The test programme was marred by a major accident in July 2000 when the fighter (flown by pilot Viktor Pugachov and WSO Roman Kondrat'yev) was on short finals to Zhukovskiy. It nearly resulted in the loss of the aircraft and crew; only Pugachov's expertise and timely information from Sukhoi CTP Igor' Votintsev, who was flying chase, saved the day, enabling the pilot to land the 'cube' in one piece. The cause of the accident and the extent of the damage were not disclosed to the press; anyway, the damage was not too bad because the aircraft was repaired and flying again by the end of the year.

In early 2001 the Su-27KUB took part in another training session on the 'unsinkable carrier' in Saki, making up for the one it missed the previous year because of the accident. It is now expected to participate in the *Admiral Kuznetsov*'s next Mediterranean cruise tentatively scheduled for the second half of 2001.

The Su-27KUB is doubtlessly a major step in the development of Russian shipboard aircraft. Despite the bigger fuselage cross-section area, it has much more refined aerodynamics than the production Su-27K. As compared to the latter aircraft; the lift/drag ratio is improved more than 10%, mainly thanks to the 'smart' adaptive wings with the 'flexible' leading edge which, together with the flaperons, continuously optimises the airfoil for maximum efficiency. The elastic LE flap seal eliminates air leaks from the wing undersurface to the upper surface. This has made the Su-27KUB extremely fuel-efficient.

Currently the Su-27KUB is powered by 'navalised' AL-31F engines featuring enhanced corrosion protection. More advanced engines (possibly Lyul'ka-Saturn AL-41Fs) may be installed later on. Besides the control surfaces (canards, stabilators, rudders, flaperons and LE flaps), the digital FBW control system governs the engines (viz, the Su-27KUB has 'power-by-wire'). This minimises trim drag and maximises lift, part of which is provided by the canards and horizontal tail.

As of this writing the Su-27KUB prototype serves as a testbed for the NIIP N-011M Bars (Leopard) fire control radar replacing the N-011 selected originally. The Zhuk-M has an increased-diameter phased array. In air-to-air mode it can track up to 20 targets within a range of 170 km (92 nm) while guiding missiles to four priority threats. In air-to-surface mode the Zhuk-M enables the aircraft to effectively destroy ground targets and surface ships 25 to 300 km (13.5 to 162 nm) away.

A unique digital processor with a speed of several dozen billion operations per second has been developed in Russia specially for the Su-27KUB and is undergoing tests as of this writing. The aircraft's new avionics architecture and the use of state-of-the-art electronic components have cut avionics weight several times as compared to the Su-27K (Su-33) while increasing the suite's capabilities. The Su-27KUB's multi-channel data processing and display system will give the crew a 360° field of view as regards aerial targets, providing complete situational

Above: The Su-27KUB leaves the T-2 ski jump of the 'unsinkable carrier' at Novofyodorovka AB, Saki.

Above and centre: The Su-27 comes in for a carrier landing in Saki.

This page and opposite:
The Su-27 during trials at
Novofyodorovka AB.

This page and opposite: More views of the Su-27KUB. These photos clearly show the fighter's 'patchwork' appearance.

With the arrestor hook deployed, the 'little cube' is on short finals to the training complex in Saki. Note the two-section trailing-edge flaps inboard of the wing folding joint.

Above: The Su-27KUB taxies after landing in Zhukovskiy. The aircraft rolled slowly along the taxiway, allowing the spectators to get a good look at it and take pictures.

The Su-27KUB tied down on the flight deck of RNS *Admiral Kuznetsov* during trials.

The Su-27KUB moments after landing on the carrier...

...and about to begin its take-off run.

This page and opposite: The Su-27KUB comes in and catches the wire on the *Admiral Kuznetsov.*

The Su-27KUB on the carrier's deck...

...and on the hardstand at Novofyodorovka AB with a 'regular' Su-27K parked behind it.

In a few minutes the naval trainer will take off from the carrier on yet another test flight.

Afterburners blazing, the Su-27KUB clears the ski jump of the *Admiral Kuznetsov*.

Above: Two views of the Su-27 in Saki following modifications. Note the position of the boarding ladder.

The ninth and final Su-27K prototype (T10K-9, c/n 49051003604).
The rudders painted completely in Russian flag colours are unique to this example.

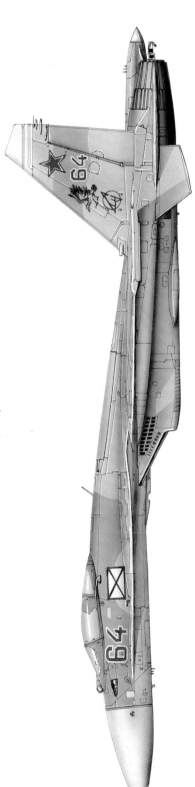

A production 279th KIAP Su-33 (Su-27K), RNS *Admiral Kuznetsov.*
Unlike the prototypes, production examples had red tactical codes;
note the different sty e of the Russian Navy flag.

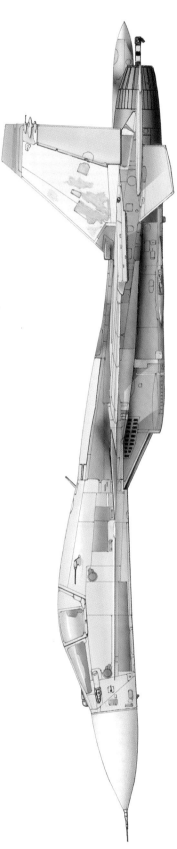

The prototype of the Su-27KUB multi-role two-seat shipboard fighter.

119

The Su-27KUB passes overhead after taking off from the T-2 ski jump in Saki.

Side view of the Su-27KUB's forward fuselage. Note the large gun blast panel.

awareness. The super-processor will give the fire control radar extremely high resolution, simplifying the design at the same time.

Data presentation systems and controls received special attention when the Su-27KUB's cockpit was designed. The 'little cube' makes use of the 'dark cockpit' principle – ie, if everything is normal the aircraft's systems do not distract the crew with warning lights. For the same reason the number of buttons, switches etc. has been kept to a minimum, allowing the crew to concentrate on the mission. For the time being both a traditional control stick and a sidestick are under consideration; a special trials programme will be held in order to make the selection.

The electronic flight instrumentation system is still being defined. As of now the common instrument panel is to feature five indigenous colour MFDs (one 21" display in the centre and four 15" displays). A helmet-mounted display (HMD) is now under development; integrating it into the Su-27KUB will allow the engineers to dispense with the usual HUDs.

The Su-27KUB is the first Russian fighter to have a liquid oxygen converter which can also generate gaseous nitrogen. This reduces the need for ground (shipboard) support equipment and maintenance personnel. Sukhoi engineers believe the aircraft will be much easier to maintain than other members of the Flanker family.

Despite its 'combat trainer' designation, the Su-27KUB is a true multi-role combat aircraft capable of fulfilling a wide range of missions – from shooting down enemy aircraft (including such difficult targets as AWACS aircraft) to destroying ground targets and surface ships with precision weapons. The GSh-301 cannon is retained for use against less important targets such as small vessels, among other things. (In short, to quote a 1970s McDonnell Douglas ad for the F-15, 'shoots down whatever's up, blows up whatever's down'.)

The *koobik* is to be developed into several new versions, including a dedicated reconnaissance aircraft and a shipboard mini-AWACS (the latter is now under development). According to preliminary reports, the AWACS version will have a fat tail 'stinger' housing the surveillance radar set; the phased-array antenna will be located in an elongated pylon-mounted pod above the fuselage, in the manner of the Ericsson PS890 Erieye radar of the SAAB 340AEW and the Embraer EMB-145.SA. This will require the fins to be made of composites so as not to impair radar operation.

The Su-27KUB may prove attractive for the Air Force as well, since its unique short-field performance enables it to operate from short tactical airstrips. The 'landlubber' version (designated Su-30K2) is described in Chapter 2.

Summing Up

Recent years have shown an alarming tendency: the Russian Air Force's equipment fleet is growing increasingly geriatric. According to the Russian Air Force General HQ, 48% of the fixed-wing and rotary-wing aircraft have been in service for 15 years or more, 23% of the fleet is ten to fifteen years old, 28% is five to ten years old and only one percent (!) of the fleet is newer. Worse, due to funding shortfalls the Air Force is having trouble keeping its aircraft operational. In 2001 the proportion of fully operational aircraft declined somewhat as compared to 1999, dropping to 56% in the Air Force's tactical arm (FA – *Frontovaya aviahtsiya*). Little is done to remedy this, since the capacity of the Air Force's aircraft overhaul plants is used only 27% – again because the military have no money to pay for refurbishment. Defence experts predict that the tactical aircraft currently on strength will have trouble remaining active until 2010.

Considering this, the statement made on 6th March 2001 was a sensation. On that day, several upgraded combat aircraft were shown to Russian Air Force C-in-C Army Gen Anatoliy Kornookov, Deputy C-in-C (Arms) Lt Gen Yuriy P. Klishin, 4th TsBP i PLS CO Maj Gen Aleksandr Kharchevskiy, Russian Army Aviation representatives, high-ranking Sukhoi OKB and IAPO officers and the media in Zhukovskiy. After inspecting the jets and helicopters Kornookov said that 'the Russian Air Force has finally begun to really update its combat aircraft'.

The aircraft on show included the prototype of the Su-27UBM combat trainer (*oochebno-boyevoy* [*samolyot*], *modernizeerovannyy* – combat-capable trainer, upgraded). Coded 20 Red and based in Akhtoobinsk, the aircraft belonged to the 929th GLITs; it had been modified by IAPO to meet an order placed by the Russian Air Force. Outwardly the aircraft was just a run-of-the-mill Flanker-C; yet it featured an upgraded avionics suite similar to that of the Su-30KN '302 Blue'. (Speaking of which, the latter aircraft was also on display.)

The upgrade enables the Su-27UBM to use a wider range of weapons; options include up to six Kh-29T TV-guided ASMs or KAB-1500Kr 'smart bombs', two Kh-59M TV-guided tactical cruise missiles, and up to six R-77 (RVV-AE) medium-range AAMs. Up to six Kh-31P anti-radiation missiles can be carried in the SEAD role, or a similar number of active radar homing Kh-31As for anti-shipping strike. The TV-guided weapons can be launched from beyond visual range; quite simply, the fire control radar downloads target information to the seeker head which then 'knows what to look for' and gets a lock-on as the missile or bomb approaches the target.

IAPO have managed to significantly enhance the Su-27UBM's counter-air capabilities merely by substituting a single display in each cockpit (it should be noted that the Russian Air Force's upgrade plans involve primarily two-seat fighters). The new MFI-55 multi-function displays show both flight information and the complete range of target data.Thus the engineers hope that retrofitting these MFDs will turn the Su-27UB and Su-30 into combat aircraft fully capable of meeting today's demands.

During the demonstration in Zhukovskiy

Russian President Vladimir V. Putin attaches great importance to the development of the nation's armed forces. Here the President is seen in the back seat of a which took him on an express trip to Chechnya in late 2000.

the Su-27UBM prototype carried a fixed acquisition round under the port wing. The round was equipped with a TV seeker head as fitted to TV-guided ASMs and 'smart bombs'. The use of such acquisition rounds makes it possible to train pilots in using precision weapons without actually using these costly munitions.

Seen here in Zhukovskiy on 6th March 2001, this is the first Su-27UB upgraded to Su-27UBM standard for the Russian Air Force.

The Su-27UBM prototype on LII's runway in Zhukovskiy.

A still from an RTR TV channel video showing Russian Air Force Su-30s being upgraded at IAPO.

This model shows how the production Su-27KUB multi-role fighter will look.

At the following press conference Army Gen Anatoliy Kornookov stated that the Russian Air Force's upgrade efforts are directed primarily at creating tactical reconnaissance/strike aircraft systems based on the types currently in service – the Su-27, Su-30, MiG-29, MiG-31, Su-24 and Su-25. Some of the aircraft to be upgraded are to operate as tactical airborne command posts or 'mini-AWACS'; the two-seat Su-30, Su-27UB and MiG-31BM are suited for this role. Kornookov went on to say that the

Russian Air Force has placed an order with IAPO for the upgrade of twenty Su-27UBs and Su-30s (the proportion is unknown – Auth.) to Su-27UBM and Su-30KN standard respectively. The first ten upgraded aircraft are to enter service in 2001.

The presentation n Zhukovskiy made the evening news on all major Russian TV channels. The reports included footage of the (still unpainted) Su-30KN prototype, 302 Blue, destroying a surface ship with a TV-guided bomb and shooting down a target drone with an R-77 AAM. Scenes from the assembly shops at IAPO showing in-service Su-30s of the 148th TsBP i PLS at Savostleyka undergoing conversion were also shown.

On 27th April 2001 AVPK Sukhoi and the Sukhoi OKB celebrated the 20th anniversary of the first flight of the T10-7 – the prototype of the future production Su-27 Flanker-B which differed a lot from the preceding T-10 prototypes (it took to the air on 20th April 1981 at the hands of former Sukhoi chief test pilot Vladimir S. Il'yushin). To mark the occasion Sukhoi demonstrated two aircraft to company employees, high-ranking Russian MoD officials and the press in Zhukovskiy; these were the T10M-11 (aka Su-37), which had been modified by then, and the first pre-production Su-30MK (Su-30MKI), 05 Blue. Built by IAPO, the latter aircraft had been displayed earlier at the Aero India'2000 airshow in Bangalore.

The demo flight of the upgraded Su-37 was performed by Sukhoi test pilot Sergey Vaschchook (who succeeded the famous test pilot Yevgeniy Frolov as Su-37 project test pilot) and made a lasting impression on the invited guests and press. The fact is, the Sukhoi OKB has done some radical rethinking of the fighter's concept, replacing the thrust-vectoring AL-31FP engines installed hitherto with regular AL-31Fs as fitted to standard production Su-27s. Concurrently, however, changes were made to the flight control system so that all control surfaces are included into a common control circuit; this, together with the installation of new indigenous avionics replacing the earlier French Sextant Avionique equipment, gave fantastic results. The modification was completed back in the summer of 2000, the aircraft making its first post-conversion flight in early October with Sergey Vaschchook at the controls. His demo flight on 27th April was so impressive that many of the invited guests at the jubilee (namely Sukhoi OKB specialists) said that the substitution of thrust-vectoring engines with ordinary ones did not impair the Su-37's capabilities in the slightest. Vaschchook performed nearly all aerobatics manoeuvres which Yevgeniy Frolov performed in the pre-conversion aircraft at various international airshows.

As for the new avionics, the changes concerned mainly the navigation system and

The updated T10M-11 (Su-37) with non-thrust-vectoring AL-31F engines (note nozzle position) at the demonstration held on 27th April 2001.

The rear end of the T10M-11 (Su-37) after re-engining with AL-31Fs.

Centre and above: Two views of the cockpit of the upgraded T10M-11 (Su-37) with three MFDs developed by the Ramenskoye Instrument Design Bureau. Note the sidestick in the lower photo.

the electronic flight instrumentation system (EFIS). Imported components were replaced by Russian-made ones; for example, the three colour MFDs (two in the centre of the instrument panel and one on the port console) have been developed by the Ramenskoye Instrument Design Bureau (RPKB) led by General Director Givi Djandjgava.

As already mentioned, the other aircraft demonstrated on 27th April was the first pre-production Su-30MK. It is powered by production thrust-vectoring AL-31FPs. Test pilots Vyacheslav Aver'yanov and Igor' Votintsev gave a spirited aerobatics display in this aircraft. The Su-30MK's front cockpit features three colour liquid-crystal MFDs (by comparison, the Chinese version, the Su-30MKK, has two). This enables the pilot to use one of them for monitoring weapons status, using the others for monitoring the tactical sutiation, feeding data to other aircraft during concerted action, selecting ECM equipment, entering target and navigation inputs. Additionally, the displays back up for each other; if one fails during a mission, the others can display all required data, increasing the chances of mission success. The second pre-production Su-30MK (04 Blue), likewise manufactured by IAPO, was in the Sukhoi OKB's hangar in Zhukovskiy at the time.

In the spring of 2001 the *Nezavisimoye voyennoye obozreniye* (Independent Military Review) published some interesting details of the Su-30MK. As reported previously, the upgrade centers on the installation of new avionics which are exclusively designed and manufactured by Russian companies having both experience in this field and state licences to develop such equipment. These include RPKB, NIIP, Gheofizika-ART, the Aviaavtomatika OKB, OKB Omega (*Osoboye konstrooktorskoye byuro* – Special Design Bureau) from Novgorod, and TsKBA (*Tsentrahl'noye konstrooktorskoye byuro avtomahtiki* – Central Design Bureau of Automatic Equipment). The new avionics utilize state-of-the-art electronic components. Virtually all of the new avionics systems consist of line-replaceable units (LRUs) and incorporate automatic built-in test equipment (BITE).

All in all the Su-30MK features no fewer than 150 new electronic modules. Changes have been made to the SUV-P WCS (*sistema oopravleniya vo'oroozheniyem*) with the BTsVM486 processor (*bortovaya tsifrovaya vychislitel'naya mashina* – on-board digital processor) enabling the aircraft to use high-precision air-to-surface weapons, the SUO-30PK armament control system (*sistema oopravleniya oroozhiyem*) governing the launch of all available weapons from all hardpoints; the aircraft features a new Model 52Sh IRST/LR unit with enhanced

The first pre-production Su-30MK 'burns rubber' at touchdown, with the brake parachutes just beginning to deploy.

White phototheodolite calibration markings were applied to the radome of the pre-production Su-30MK in the course of the trials.

The front cockpit of the first pre-production Su-30MK (05 Blue).

eters are automatically fed into the avionics by means of a flash memory card in the BRP-3 data recorder (*blok reghi**strah**tsii parahmetrov*).

As previously discussed, the open avionics architecture is one of the main strong points of the Su-30MK's updated avionics suite, allowing the fighter's capabilities to be expanded without major changes – in fact, just by adding or replacing an equipment module. For instance, to give the radar air-to-surface capability and make it compatible with the Kh-31A anti-shipping missile the aircraft needs to be retrofitted with just three new modules; no other changes to the avionics are required. After that, only around 30 test flights are required to make the aircraft fully combat-capable, which allows a production plant (for example, IAPO) to easily launch production of a multi-role fighter capable of anti-surface ship warfare (ASuW).

The Sukhoi OKB and IAPO also plan to offer the Su-30MK with the ARM-TSV automated test and data processing system which enables flight and mission profiles to be deciphered, using a variety of parameters to evaluate mission efficiency, as well as a

capabilities, the Berkoot (Golden Eagle) video recording system (today's answer to the old gun camera), the L150 unit (most probably an active jammer), the Soora-K helmet-mounted sight (HMS), the Tekon guid-ance pod for the Kh-59ME TV-guided AGM, and a new flight data recorder.

The new equipment cuts mission preparation/turnaround time and allows missions to be better prepared, since the mission param-

Rear view of Su-30MK '05 Blue' with the airbrake deployed. Note how the vectoring nozzles of the AL-31FU engines point inwards as they turn down; the rotation axes are tilted, providing a side force (and thus directional TVC) during differential deflection of the nozzles.

computerised simulator system for training air and ground crews.

Currently the Russian Air Force can hardly afford the expensive Su-30MK. Moreover, some high-ranking Russian MoD and government officials are less than enthusiastic about ordering Generation 4+ fighters, believing it would make more sense to spend money on fifth-generation combat aircraft. Still, the Su-30MK is duly tested by the Russian Air Force's State Flight Test Centre (929th GLITs), as are the Su-30MKK, Su-35UB and other export versions. For one thing, manufacturers are not exactly impartial about their products; thus, having the Air Force perform an independent test programme saves Russia the possible embarrassment of offering substandard goods to foreign customers (the military traditionally have the final word, since the aircraft are designed to meet their demands). On the other hand, government policies (and officials) may change; and a proponent of 'pie-in-the-sky' projects may be replaced by an official supporting more down-to-earth but readily implementable programmes.

As for 'clean sheet of paper' projects of tactical aircraft, Kornookov says large-scale deliveries of new-generation aircraft to tactical aviation units will not begin until 2008 or 2010. A notable exception is the Su-27IB multi-mission strike aircraft, as the Su-34/Su-32FN will be known when it enters service (it is already referred to by the Russian Air Force as such); the first production examples will be delivered to first-line units during 2002-2003.

Meanwhile, one of the 'big head Flankers' has been delivered to the Russian Air Force for evaluation. An upgraded version of the Su-27IB (Su-34) is due to enter flight test shortly; it will feature more advanced avionics (most probably an improved WCS built around the abovementioned new fire control radar replacing the V-004).

The bottom line is that, thanks to the enormous growth potential of the original Su-27 interceptor and the fruitful co-operation between the airframers, engine designers and avionics specialists (both R&D establishments and manufacturers), Russia's air arm will soon receive a uniquely versatile combat aircraft family which will bolster its capabilities considerably.

Speaking of all-new designs, currently the Russian 'fighter makers' (Sukhoi,

Sukhoi OKB test pilot Vyacheslav Aver'yanov seen in the cockpit of a pre-production Su-30MK.

Mikoyan and Yakovlev) are working on the LFS (*lyohkiy frontovoy samolyot* – light tactical aircraft) fifth-generation fighter programme. Importantly, many Russian industry and defence experts believe that while the LFS will be developed on a competitive basis, the winning design will be produced and marketed as a joint effort.

Pre-production Su-30MK '05 Blue' is towed back to the Sukhoi hangar after a demonstration flight on 27th April 2001.

ILYUSHIN IL-76
Russia's Versatile Airlifter

Yefim Gordon & Dmitriy Komissarov

The Soviet Union's answer to the Lockheed Starlifter first flew in 1971 and has become familiar both in its intended military guise and as a commercial freighter. It has also been developed as the IL-78 for aerial refuelling, and in AEW and other versions.

There is not only a full development history and technical description, but extensive tables detailing each aircraft built, with c/n, serial and so on, and detailed notes on every operator, both civil and military, and their fleets.

Softback, 280 x 215 mm, 160 pages
c250 b/w and colour photos, drawings
1 85780 106 7   **£19.95/US $34.95**

Aerofax
MIKOYAN-GUREVICH MiG-15

Yefim Gordon

In this Aerofax, compiled from a wealth of first-hand Russian sources, there is a comprehensive history of every evolution of the Soviet Union's swept-wing fighter and its service. Notably in this volume, there are tables listing intricate details of many individual aircraft, a concept which would have been unthinkable in any publications only a few years ago.

There is extensive and detailed photo coverage, again from Russian sources, almost all of which is previously unseen.

Softback, 280 x 215 mm, 160 pages
211 b/w, 18 colour photos, 7pp colour sideviews , 18pp b/w drawings
1 85780 105 9   **£17.95/US $29.95**

SUKHOI S-37 & MIKOYAN MFI
Russian Fifth-Generation
Fighter Technology Demonstrators

Yefim Gordon

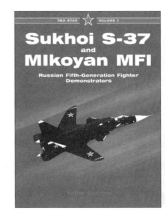

Conceived as an answer to the American ATF programme, the Mikoyan MFI (better known as the 1.42 or 1.44) and the Sukhoi S-37 Berkoot were developed as technology demonstrators. Both design bureaux used an approach that was quite different from Western fifth-generation fighter philosophy. This gives a detailed account of how these enigmatic aircraft were designed, built and flown. It includes structural descriptions of both types.

Sbk, 280 x 215 mm, 96pp plus gatefold
182 b/w and colour photographs, drawings/side-views
1 85780 120 2   **£17.95/US $27.95**

SOVIET COMBAT AIRCRAFT OF THE SECOND WORLD WAR
Volume One: Single-Engined Fighters
Yefim Gordon and Dmitri Khazanov

Arranged by manufacturer, this includes the prototype and operational products of famous designers such as Lavochkin, Mikoyan and Yakovlev as well as the lesser known, such as the Bereznyak-Isaev rocket propelled fighter.

Rich Russian sources including manufacturers, flight test establishments and Soviet air force and naval aviation records provide a wealth of new material, much of which rewrites previously held Western views.

Hardback, 282 x 213 mm, 184 pages
358 b/w photos; 28 layout diagrams,
16 full colour side views
1 85780 083 4   **£24.95/US $39.95**

SOVIET COMBAT AIRCRAFT OF THE SECOND WORLD WAR
Twin Eng Fighters, Attack Acft & Bombers
Yefim Gordon and Dmitri Khazanov

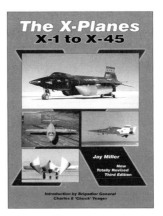

Arranged by designer, this includes the products of famous names such as Ilyushin, Petlyakov and Tupolev as well as lesser known types.

In his introduction, Bill Gunston explains the unique nature of Soviet aviation, the politics and strategies and the problems created by the vastness of the country – and confirms that the two volumes of *Soviet Combat Aircraft* are set to become the premier reference on this facet of aviation history.

Hardback, 282 x 213 mm, 176 pages
285 b/w photos; 27 layout diagrams;
17 full colour side views
1 85780 084 2   **£24.95/US $39.95**

THE X-PLANES X-1 to X-45
New, totally revised third edition

Jay Miller

This new, totally revised and updated version of 'The X-Planes' contains a detailed and authoritative account of every single X-designated aircraft. There is considerable new, and newly-declassified information on all X-Planes.

Each aircraft is described fully with coverage of history, specifications, propulsion systems and disposition. Included are rare cockpit illustrations. Each X-Plane is also illustrated by a detailed multi-view drawing.

Hardback, 280 x 216mm, 440 pages
c850 b/w, 52 colour photographs,
approximately 110 drawings
1 85780 109 1   **£39.95/US $59.95**

SOVIET X-PLANES

Yefim Gordon & Bill Gunston

A detailed review of Soviet experimental aircraft from the early 1900s through to the latest Russian prototypes of today.

The book is the first to collect the stories of the more important Soviet experimental aircraft into one volume. Working from original sources the authors have produced an outstanding reference which although concentrating on hardware also includes many unflown projects. About 150 types are described, each with relevant data, and including many three-view drawings.

Hardback, 282 x 213mm, 240 pages
355 b/w, 50 colour photos; 200 dwgs
1 85780 099 0   **£29.95/US $44.95**